NEBS
MANAGEMENT
DEVELOPMENT
SUPER SERIES

User Guide

Published for

&NEBS Management *by*

Pergamon
Flexible
Learning

Pergamon Flexible Learning
An imprint of Butterworth-Heinemann
Linacre House, Jordan Hill, Oxford OX2 8DP
225 Wildwood Avenue, Woburn, MA 01801-2041
A division of Reed Educational and Professional Publishing Ltd

 A member of the Reed Elsevier plc group

OXFORD   AUCKLAND   BOSTON
JOHANNESBURG   MELBOURNE   NEW DELHI

First published 1997
Reprinted 2000 (twice)

British Library Cataloguing in Publication Data
A catalogue record for this book is available from the British Library

ISBN 0 7506 3705 6

The views expressed in this work are those
of the authors and do not necessarily reflect
those of the National Examining Board for
Supervision and Management or of the publisher.

NEBS Management Project Manager: Diana Thomas
Author: David Pardey
Editor: Ian Bloor
Composition by Genesis Typesetting, Rochester, Kent
Printed and bound in Great Britain

Contents

1 Introduction 1
   1.1 Welcome 1
   1.2 For whom is this *User Guide* intended? 2

2 About Super Series 5

3 Using Super Series 7
   3.1 Introduction 7
   3.2 How the workbooks are structured 7
   3.3 Getting the most from the workbooks 20
   3.4 How the audio cassettes are structured 22
   3.5 Getting the most from the cassettes 23

4 Routes to capability and competence 27
   4.1 Introduction 27
   4.2 Learning methods 28
   4.3 Capability awards 29
   4.4 Competence awards 34

5 Managing your learning 40
   5.1 Introduction 40
   5.2 Flexible learning 41
   5.3 Learning to learn 42
   5.4 Planning your learning 45
   5.5 Your personal development plan 46

6 Help and support 48
   6.1 Introduction 48
   6.2 Using internal support 48
   6.3 Using external support 51
   6.4 Support from NEBS Management 51
   6.5 Taking your personal development further 52

Appendix 1 Summary of workbook contents 55

Appendix 2 Summary of audio cassette contents 62

Appendix 3 Sources of general help and advice 66

1 Introduction

1.1 Welcome

Welcome to the Super Series and to the Super Series *User Guide*. You are about to find out about the:

- 40 workbooks
- 5 audio cassettes

which make up the third edition of the best-selling Super Series flexible learning materials.

This *User Guide* will tell you all you need to know about:

- for whom the Super Series is intended and what it contains;
- what each of the workbooks and cassettes in the series is about;
- how you can use the workbooks and the other materials which support them;
- how you can be assessed and achieve nationally recognized qualifications;
- how you should plan your learning;
- what extra help is available, and how to use it.

You should read through the whole of this guide carefully before you start your study programme. If you have used flexible learning materials before, you will probably have some idea what Super Series is like, but time spent now learning about all the features will be of enormous value to you, and is the best way to make a start.

By the end of this *User Guide* you will be better able to plan and control your own learning using Super Series and be able to take maximum advantage of the flexibility that this approach offers. It's called 'flexible learning' because you learn flexibly

- **when** you want
- **where** you want
- **how** you want to learn.

It might be during work time, after work or at weekends, or it might be a combination of these. You can use Super Series at work – in your own workplace or in a special Centre set aside for learning. You can use it at home – in your kitchen or sitting room, on the dining table or wherever you can be left to work in peace and quiet. You might be using it at a college, a public library or a specialist training centre, where there are many other people using similar types of workbooks on a range of different topics.

1

You will find that you are encouraged to use your own workplace to apply what you have learnt, either now or (if you are not currently in employment) in the future. This is because experience is one of the best teachers, and you can't learn about the practice of management without it! The *User Guide* also focuses strongly on the way that you should plan your learning and integrate it into your work. It encourages you to think about what you need to learn and how and when you need to learn it, and emphasizes the value of the support available to you and the need to take advantage of it in ways that match your particular needs.

Above all else, this *User Guide* is designed to help **you**. Whether you are new to flexible learning or have used the approach before, the *User Guide* will ensure that you get the best out of the learning materials, which is why you should take some time to read through it, and keep it by you throughout your programme.

1.2 For whom is this *User Guide* intended?

Nearly thirty years ago Lawrence Appley said that a manager was someone 'who gets things done through other people'. You may lead a team of two or twenty, you may report to another manager or direct to the owner or chief executive. You might have held this position, or one just like it, for many years as a full-time or part-time employee or, on the other hand, you may be looking forward to employment or promotion into just such a role. Whatever your situation it will be your responsibility to ensure that those who work for you do so effectively and efficiently.

Your job title might be:

- Supervisor
- Team Leader
- Office Manager
- Ward Sister or Charge Nurse
- Chief Technician

Job titles aren't all that important; what matters is that you want to learn about the theory and practice of managing a group of people better, a group of people that you have direct responsibility for and a group of people actively involved in making a product or delivering a service. This is *first line management*, and that is what the Super Series is all about. It is designed both for those in post and those looking for their first step into a managerial position. It doesn't assume that you currently supervise anybody else, but it does assume that you look forward to having just such a responsibility.

If you are already in post you may have learnt a lot about the role and have acquired skills and knowledge from a variety of different sources – courses, personal experience and observation, reading, etc. – but don't assume that means you will be able to skim through the workbooks without any effort. If you feel you are already competent, you will find that the workbooks will encourage you to think more deeply about your role and the way that you undertake it. This 'reflection' is a central element of good learning, encouraging you to think about not just what you do, but why you do it and how well you do it (something which is looked at in some detail in Chapter 3).

If you are completely new to the first line management role, and looking forward to having the opportunity to put Super Series into practice, you will find that there are a variety of different tasks and activities which put what you are learning about into context, helping you to practise and test your learning. You can then reflect on what you have learnt and what you still need to learn or to do in order to develop yourself and your performance.

The world of work is changing fast and Super Series has had to move into a third edition in response. For example, there are types of organization existing today which didn't exist at all when the first Super Series was published:

- direct labour organizations contracting with local councils to build roads or remove waste
- self-managing schools and colleges
- mobile telephone and cable TV companies
- Internet service providers
- World Wide Web page designers.

You might work for an organization like this; it might be in the public, private or voluntary sector, operating *for profit* or *not for profit* – Super Series is designed to support all these different types of employment. You might work for a manufacturing company, and so there are examples drawn from manufacturing – but equally you might work in a hospital, a school or a charity shop, so Super Series covers all types of organizations in all types of activities, from agriculture to zoos!

You could be using Super Series to learn about just one aspect of first line management – team-building or costing, perhaps – without any qualification aim. Alternatively you could be working towards one of several different awards, either through Super Series alone, or in combination with other types of activity. This could be a full qualification, one NEBS Management Certificate Module or S/NVQ Unit, or you could be using Super Series to revise or catch up on a course. This is why, in Chapter 2, we will help you choose the right workbooks for you and in Chapter 4, we will look at the qualifications which you could find yourself working towards.

Whoever you are, whatever your employment position, you are embarking on a programme which is both demanding and rewarding, and you will need to manage your learning and take advantage of any support available. In Chapter 5 you will be encouraged to plan your work, set yourself targets and establish agreed routines so that you are able to achieve these targets without disruption or anxiety, and if you have the help of others you should take full advantage of it to maximize your chances of success.

What sort of help might you get?

- Some employers run their own training or resource centres, with specialist staff to help you.
- You may have access to a College of Further or Higher Education, a University or a private training organization.
- There may be a public library which operates an Open Learning Centre, where you can go to undertake some of the further reading that you will find mentioned or simply to find somewhere quiet and peaceful to work away from distractions.

Use these facilities, they are there to help you.

If you do have access to a Learning Resource Centre you should find that it contains a very wide range of facilities designed to help you to learn, including:

- text-based resources (like this!);
- audio and video resources (which are also contained within Super Series) and playback facilities for them;
- computer-based resources, including everything from simple instructional packages to interactive CD-ROMs and online services such as the Internet.

Using these support systems and facilities is the subject of Chapter 6. Don't be put off if they are not familiar to you, because there will undoubtedly be someone to help you use them. If you're not experienced with computers or if you have any specific problems with reading or writing, or dealing with numbers, don't try to hide them or, worse still, give up, because there will probably be resources available to help you with your problems.

Equally, if you have any disabilities which present difficulties for you in engaging in learning, you will find that flexible learning with Super Series is ideal for you. Because you can work at your own pace and in a place that suits you, you should have no problems with access or participation in a programme – whatever your background, whatever your goals, Super Series is designed to help you!

2 About Super Series

There are forty Super Series workbooks and five audio cassette tapes giving you a substantial degree of choice about which ones to work with. The full list of materials with a summary of their content appears in the Appendices, but before you take a look it is useful to understand how they are organized. To help you, all the workbook titles are grouped into four areas, reflecting the structure of the S/NVQs in Management and the modules of the NEBS Management Certificate. These are:

Managing Activities
Managing Resources
Managing People
Managing Information

Because each workbook and cassette is totally self-contained and covers a complete topic you can start with any one you like and choose further ones in any order. For a small number of workbooks it can be useful to complete one before another (examples are *Planning Training and Development* before *Delivering Training* and *Understanding Quality* before *Achieving Quality*) but it's best to select an order which makes sense to you in your work role or employment ambitions, and gives you some variety and stimulation as you work through. Each workbook starts with a *study links* diagram (there is more on these on page 8) which will help you in building up a logical and coherent order. You should also consider your purpose in using Super Series (whether or not you are aiming for a qualification, details of which are explained in Chapter 4) and your current experience and role.

The new edition of Super Series reflects the many changes that have taken place in the world of work over the past few years, and in particular the role of first line managers. The emphasis is clearly on the variety of roles that you could be performing, in the private, public or voluntary sectors and in manufacturing or service industries. It puts a lot of emphasis on the issues that are clearly concerning most employers these days, and especially concerns about:

- competition and responsiveness to the market;
- quality and choice to meet the needs of individuals;
- working in teams to improve the efficiency and effectiveness of operations;
- reducing layers of management and delegating responsibility for financial control and decision-making as far down the organization as possible;
- meeting external demands for accountability and the increasingly complex legal framework and environmental regulations within which organizations operate;
- internationalism, both towards the European Union and wider afield towards the Far East and Pacific region.

Collectively this content covers all the knowledge and understanding required for NEBS Management's:

- Introductory Award
- Certificate
- S/NVQ in Management at Level 3

Furthermore, the special portfolio activities and the Work-based assignment that the workbooks ask you to undertake will help you to gather possible acceptable evidence for your S/NVQ portfolio.

Before we move on to Chapter 3, to look at how the workbooks and cassettes are structured, you might find it useful to spend a few minutes looking at Appendix 1, to get some idea of the range of topics covered.

3 Using Super Series

3.1 Introduction

This section of the *User Guide* tells you how the workbooks and audio cassette tapes are structured so that once you start you will recognize the various components and know how to get the best from your efforts. Each one contains various elements designed to help you to learn, to check that you have learnt correctly, and to guide you into applying that learning. The time that you spend in reading through this section will be time well spent, as you will then find that you can start with confidence.

We don't assume that you know anything about the topic when you start, but we do encourage you to think about what you do know and can already do, so that you build on that. Everybody knows far more than they give themselves credit for, and the activities and tasks that you will come across are important in helping you to recognize your existing learning and fit new ideas into that network of skills and knowledge. Since the resource material has been written without having met you personally, we ask you to add those items that relate to your own experience so that you can feel that you are contributing to the process of learning just as much as we do.

3.2 How the workbooks are structured

Before reading about the structure of a Super Series workbook you should make sure that you have one available, so that you can see what it is we are referring to.

You will find that each workbook is just under 100 pages long – not so big that it presents too much of a challenge, nor so short that it can only skim over the topics it covers. It is designed to take you between eight and ten hours to complete, and later on you will be encouraged to plan how you will organize those 8–10 hours with the resources available to help you.

Each workbook is divided up into four main parts:

Introduction	Covers the objectives and introduces the topic
Sessions	Main content of the workbook, containing explanations, case studies, activities and feedback, questions, and self-assessments

Performance checks	Checks what you have understood and helps you apply it to your own job
Reflect and review	Helps you think back over what you have learnt, check your answers to tests and self-assessments and plan how you might apply what you have learnt to the future.

There are also some symbols (called *icons*) associated with some of the elements in the workbook; these help to identify the particular element and encourage you to recognize what you are expected to do. The rest of this section will describe these elements (and the icons) in more detail, starting with the *introduction*.

You will soon realize that the most significant feature of all the workbooks in Super Series is that they are not *text*books but *work*books. In other words, you don't just read them, but use them to help you learn and *change* the way you work. You will find that they don't just tell you about management, they also ask you – what you think about an idea or practice, what you would do in a given set of circumstances, and why you think or act in that way. The workbooks are designed to influence your way of working, helping you to identify good practice and understand why some ways of working are better than others. They should also help you to understand better the decisions made by others, such as colleagues and senior managers, and be better informed about the way that organizations work.

The workbook introduction

This consists of:

Study links	Links you to other Super Series third edition workbooks
S/NVQ links	Links you to MCI standards
Workbook objectives	Introduces the topic and tells you what you will be able to achieve by the end of the workbook
Activity planner	Points you to those activities that may require some planning

Study links

You can use as many or as few Super Series workbooks as you wish and study them in any order, but it's useful to know how each book links with others, so that you can choose those that suit your own personal requirements. Sometimes it is very useful to know about the contents of other workbooks to put something into context or to deal with the sort of real-life situations that you might encounter.

Study links are in the form of a 'honeycomb' diagram; find the one at the beginning of your workbook. The circle in the middle contains the name of the workbook you are currently working through; around it are four hexagonal shapes with the names of the four main groups of workbooks:

Managing Activities
Managing Resources
Managing People
Managing Information

Linked to each of these four group headings are circles with the names of the workbooks or audio cassettes in that group which have links with this one (if there are any). These links may be that they deal with related matter (*Achieving Quality* and *Understanding Quality*, for example) or they may deal with a topic which contributes a related set of skills or knowledge (*Delegating Effectively* and *Solving Problems*, for example). Appendix 1 gives an outline of the content of all the workbooks to help you plan your programme and understand better the importance of these links.

S/NVQ links

Each workbook supports specific elements of the Scottish and National Vocational Qualifications (S/NVQs) in Management at Level 3; how they do this is explained in the introduction to each workbook. If you are preparing an assessment portfolio, the S/NVQ links will assist you with your portfolio planning, helping you relate to specific S/NVQ elements and personal competences in which you wish to develop and demonstrate your competence.

Workbook objectives

This part tells you what your workbook covers by describing what you should know and be able to do by the time you have reached the end of the workbook. This is the most important part for you, because it doesn't simply say that you will 'know about' something, it says you will be able to *explain* ..., *decide* ..., *recognize* ..., *encourage* ..., *lead* ..., etc.

Look at a typical set of objectives in your workbook and you will see that it describes the sort of performance that you can expect from yourself on completion. It sets you a challenge to read the workbook and complete the various activities, to change or improve the way you work, and, perhaps above all, to relate better to other people.

Activity planner

This is placed at the end of the introduction, before you start the first session, to alert you to any of the activities in the workbook for which some advance planning is needed. This may involve you arranging to discuss something with your manager, or identifying a particular problem which will be the basis of an extended study throughout the workbook. You might need to start collecting information from the workplace or copies of specific organizational documents, such as a Health and Safety policy. Some of this planning will involve you in specific activities; sometimes it will require you to think about a particular activity or practice. Whichever it is, the advance notice is there for a purpose, to help you learn effectively and to use your time economically, so don't ignore it or 'mean to do it later' – plan when and how you will do it when you reach the section and before you continue with the workbook.

The workbook sessions

Following the introduction you will find the next part of the workbook divided up into several *sessions* (Session A, Session B, etc.). There are usually three or four sessions making up the complete workbook and each will take around two to three hours to complete. Each session consists of different elements designed to help you learn effectively. These are:

Text and graphics   The main topic discussions, case studies and cameos, illustrations and diagrams

Activities and feedback Confirming your learning

Portfolio activities   Self-assessment evidence development exercises

Margin notes   Notes, anecdotes, definitions, quotes and sayings

Extensions   References to further reading and follow-up

Self-assessments   Short end of session test

Summary   Summary of key learning points

Each element is there for a purpose so don't skip over any of them because you think that they aren't important or that they are too easy – if they are there they are important, and if they are too easy are you sure that you have really understood the question?

Text and graphics

Unlike many standard textbooks, Super Series workbooks talk **to** you not **at** you, just like this *User Guide*. They have been written by people skilled both in the subject matter and in the style required for flexible learning, so that you shouldn't find them difficult to read. They have diagrams to show you how ideas and practices link together and examples drawn from real life to illustrate the topic.

There will also be plenty of lists, diagrams and tables to help you understand and recognize what and how something should be done.

Activities

Activities play a major part in your understanding of each session by:

■ helping you to test how well you have understood something you have just read (*progress checking*);

■ encouraging you to think about (reflect on) something and plan how you can apply it (*possible evidence development*); or

■ providing a useful tool which you may be able to use at work straight away (*practical application*).

Activities are designed to help you understand, remember and apply as much of the new subject as possible. They are practical and take many different forms from straightforward questions to drawing diagrams and are designed to keep you interested and committed to your learning.

There are two types of activity to look out for: the 'normal' activity which performs the checking and testing function described above, and the 'portfolio' activity indicated by the icon shown on the left, which refers to the special activities, which you read about earlier when we looked at the activity planner, that should help you to generate competence evidence should you be undertaking a S/NVQ qualification route. You will need to discuss this with your Centre before you start assembling your portfolio, since they may have some specific requirements regarding the way that assessment evidence is assembled. There is more advice on this in Chapters 4 (on the different qualification routes) and 6 (on the support you can expect from your Centre).

Each activity has a *time guide*; if you find that you are taking far longer than the time guide suggests, you should have a word with your tutor, trainer or other adviser. A *response box* on the page provides you with the space to write your answer and gives you some idea of the size of response expected. Feedback on activities appears either in the text immediately following the response box or at the end of the workbook.

Margin notes

You will find that there are occasional notes printed in the margin; these are there to add to the text, by giving illustrations, definitions or quotations relevant to the points covered. These are sometimes humorous or unusual, but always add to your learning and set you thinking about the topic – have a look for one in your workbook. (By the way, the margin is large enough for you to write your own notes, if you find that useful!).

Extensions

These refer you to particularly relevant sources of further information; while it is not necessary for you to follow every one of these up in order to complete your course, they can expand your knowledge and understanding. The references will be to the latest or the most appropriate textbooks, videos, computer software or other publications, with details and comments about each one. Extensions appear in two places; as a brief reference in the margin alongside the text to which they refer and in fuller detail in the reflect and review section at the end.

Self-assessment

At the end of each session you will find the *self-assessment* to help you check how well you have understood the topic covered in that session. These will take a variety of forms; there will be questions requiring one word or short sentence answers, complete the missing word and multiple choice questions, and even crossword puzzles; the answers to these questions are at the end of the workbook. The self-assessment is intended for you to use as a progress check on your own learning and therefore unlikely to be used by anyone else (such as a tutor) for any other form of assessment. If you find you don't understand a question, got an answer wrong, or disagree with the answer given, you should look back over the session and try again. You are strongly advised **not** to move on to the next session until this has been done properly.

Summary

Following the self-assessment is the session *summary*. This is to remind you of the key learning points and reinforce your learning. It also acts as a bridge into the next session, so if you finish working on a session one day, and come back a few days later to start the next, you will find the summary useful in reminding you how far you have got. It will also be handy as a reminder if you want to come back to the workbook at a later stage (perhaps when a problem arises at work, or when a study link is identified in another workbook) and means you won't have to rely on just your memory. Glance through the summary of Session A in one of your workbooks now, to see what it is about.

Performance checks

Performance checks are designed to pull together all that you have learnt in the workbook. They comprise:

Quick quiz	Fifteen short questions covering the whole workbook
Workbook assessment	A case study/simulation exercise
Work-based assignment	A work-based practical exercise linked to S/NVQ and personal competences

Quick quiz

This is a series of short questions to test your recall of the main ideas you will have met during the workbook. Answers to the quick quiz appear at the end of the workbook; check your responses to the questions and if you get the answer wrong or could not answer a question, go back to the appropriate pages and work through the topic again.

Workbook assessment

This will take about one hour to complete and consists of a short case study and a series of questions asking you to analyse the situation and recommend a course of action. The exact nature of the exercise will vary according to the subject matter of the workbook. The *workbook assessment* is designed to help you to confirm what you have learnt, and will possibly be used by a tutor as a formal means of assessment towards a particular qualification (as explained in Chapter 4). This will be particularly important if you are not yet in post or don't have the opportunity to put the ideas you have learnt into practice through the work-based assignment, below.

Work-based assignment

The *work-based assignment* is a practical exercise designed to put your learning into practice. It too offers you the chance to confirm your learning, but also checks your ability to convert what you have learnt into action. The nature of this type of assignment encourages original research, problem-solving and communications skills that will be useful aids to developing your own skills as well as providing your organization with something substantial that they can benefit from. The work-based assignment will also help you with possible acceptable evidence towards a S/NVQ and personal competence development (again, this is explained in Chapter 4).

Reflect and review

Each workbook finishes with a *reflect and review* section which comprises:

Reflect and review	Review of the original workbook objectives
Action plan	Your personal plan of action
Extensions	Full details of sources of further reading
Answers to activities, self-assessments and the quick quiz	To check your learning

This section is where you can put your learning into a wider context – what you knew and could do before you started and what you will go on to learn and to do afterwards. Learning is something we should all expect to continue to do throughout our lives (*lifelong learning*), and the Super Series material will support your learning for many years to come, as you put ideas into action, deal with common events in new ways and face up to new challenges.

Reflect and review

How well have you achieved the objectives of this workbook? For example, the workbook *Understanding Quality* has as one of its objectives:

When you have completed this workbook you will be better able to explain what quality means.

In the reflect and review section you are asked two questions:

- What does quality mean exactly as far as **your** job and **your** team are concerned?
- Looking a little wider, how important would you say that quality was to your organization?

You can see that these questions go right to the heart of the objective – if you can't answer them then you probably haven't got a very good grasp on the topic. But even more important, by thinking about the question you might also start to think about ways in which you, your team and the organization need to move forward in developing a more quality-conscious strategy. The purpose of the reflect and review section is to start you thinking about how you move on beyond the workbook. Turn to the reflect and review section of a workbook and compare it to the objectives at the front to see what we mean.

Action plan

An *action plan* is not a single document, but a process through which you can think about both longer-term goals and the way you will achieve them, and regularly establish shorter-term targets and actions which will help you move towards those goals.

If you are using Super Series as part of a structured development programme, perhaps leading to a qualification, then you will probably be receiving advice, guidance and tutorial support in your programme from an organization which we will refer to as your *Centre*. This may be your employer, a university, college or a training organization; you will be encouraged by your Centre to discuss your longer-term goals when you start your programme, to see what the Centre can do to help you to achieve them. They will also be responsible for helping you to plan your assessment if you are working towards a qualification (and also for registering you with NEBS Management so that you can obtain your qualification).

You may have the opportunity to discuss your career and what direction you want it to go in over the next few years, and the range of employment opportunities available to you. If you do, you should take this opportunity as it can be valuable to discuss such issues with someone who might be able to assess the chances of you being able to achieve your goals, and give you advice on how best to achieve them.

The Centre will also be able to design a programme appropriate to your needs once it knows what these are. This will include decisions about:

- the qualification aim;
- the particular workbooks you will use, and the order you will use them in;
- the way that you are assessed and what you must do to prepare for assessment.

In setting your career goals and choosing Super Series workbooks to help you achieve them, you will find that they offer you further assistance in achieving your goals, by encouraging you to plan the individual steps along the route. Each workbook contains an action plan which will help you to help you make the maximum use of what you have learnt by turning your learning into action. If you turn to the back of your workbook you will find one laid out like the one below.

Desired outcomes			
1 Issues	2 Action	3 Resources	4 Target completion
Actual outcomes			

How are you supposed to complete this? You will frequently come across the acronym SMART in the Super Series workbooks when we talk about setting objectives. SMART means:

Specific: Don't be too vague about your desired outcomes or you will never know whether you have been successful or not.

Measurable: So that you can judge your success – have you achieved your desired outcomes or not?

Agreed: Who else is involved; have you got their co-operation or approval?

Realistic: 'Today Newport Pagnall, tomorrow the world!' Set your goals at a level you can achieve, and then re-set them, slightly higher. That's what we mean by continuous improvement.

Time-constrained: Have a clear time frame in which to achieve your goals, and don't try to plan too far ahead – often it is sensible to restrict yourself to a 90-day timespan, since that is the longest period over which you can seriously forecast what you are likely to be able to do in the detail needed by the action plan.

The action plan follows these rules. You will see that it starts by asking you to identify a goal (the *desired outcome*); this could be:

- a completed task or event;
- agreement of your team or line manager to a particular way of working;
- a change in the way of working;
- a level of output or quality of service.

Don't set desired outcomes which are too ambitious. They must be Realistic (SMART), which means that they must be within your power to achieve, but that doesn't stop you setting targets that stretch you, encouraging yourself to go beyond the usual limits that you set for yourself.

But setting targets for yourself is not enough – you must also plan how you can achieve them. The action plan helps you to do this by asking you to break the goal down into its constituent parts, called *issues*, which helps you to think about all the Specific (SMART) steps you need to take, and then working out actions you need take to make them happen. By checking off that you have undertaken the actions and then that you have achieved the desired outcomes, your objectives are Measurable (SMART). You should also identify the *resources* – the people, money, facilities or equipment – that you need to put these actions into practice and gain Agreement (SMART) to using them to achieve your objectives. Finally, you need to decide when you expect to have achieved them – the *target completion date* – so that your objectives are Time-constrained (SMART).

Let's look at an example. After working through the workbook *Delegating Effectively* you might decide that you need to encourage members of your team to take on more responsibility for managing their day-to-day work tasks, by agreeing amongst themselves who will take responsibility for each one, rather than relying on you to tell them what to do. This will give you more time to plan ahead, train individuals and undertake other tasks which you see as being important – these are your desired outcomes.

Desired outcomes			
By the end of the year members of the work team will be able to take on responsibility for decisions about allocating tasks between themselves, allowing me to spend more time on the managerial tasks that I can undertake			
1 Issues	2 Action	3 Resources	4 Target completion

What you now need to do is to decide how you are going to make this happen. It could be that you decide that the best way to start is to discuss this with your team and get their agreement to the desired outcomes. How are you going to do this? Perhaps by organizing a team meeting and preparing a briefing for the team:

Desired outcomes			
By the end of the year members of the work team will be able to take on responsibility for decisions about allocating tasks between themselves, allowing me to spend more time on the managerial tasks that I can undertake			
1 Issues	2 Action	3 Resources	4 Target completion
a team agreement	Convene team meeting Prepare briefing		

What is needed in the way of resources to enable these actions to be taken, and by when can it be done? The briefing will need a meeting room, and it can be done fairly quickly, so the target completion date is set for two weeks hence, on 1 October:

Desired outcomes			
By the end of the year members of the work team will be able to take on responsibility for decisions about allocating tasks between themselves, allowing me to spend more time on the managerial tasks that I can undertake			
1 Issues	2 Action	3 Resources	4 Target completion
a team agreement	Convene team meeting Prepare briefing	Book meeting room	In October

Following this, the complete series of issues, actions, resources and target completion dates is added to the Action plan to enable the desired outcomes to be achieved, as shown below:

Desired outcomes			
By the end of the year members of the work team will be able to take on responsibility for decisions about allocating tasks between themselves, allowing me to spend more time on the managerial tasks that I can undertake			
1 Issues	2 Action	3 Resources	4 Target completion
a team agreement	Convene team meeting Prepare briefing	Book meeting room	In October
b Identify tasks	Maintain work diary for two weeks	Nil	12th October
c Team review	Convene team meeting	Book meeting room	13th December
Actual outcomes			

What has still been left free is the final box – *actual outcomes*. What actually happened? Did you achieve your goal? Did you identify all the issues correctly? Did you undertake all the actions that you planned, and did they produce the results you had intended? Did you identify the resources that you needed, and were they available? And did you do all this by the dates that you set for yourself?

By asking yourself these questions you will learn from your mistakes as well as from your successes. If you don't review your actions, good or ill, you never progress. Some people have ten years' experience, others have one year's experience ten times! Successful people are like successful organizations; they try new ideas and they take calculated risks, always stretching their personal or corporate frontiers. If they get it wrong (and you only know you are taking risks if you make mistakes occasionally), then they can learn from that.

Failure comes from two sources:

- never trying anything new, to avoid making mistakes; and
- making the same mistakes again!

If you want to learn you must be prepared to do new things, and they won't always work first time. If you reflect on why it went wrong (or why it went right, for that matter) and feed back that information to improve future performance, then you are really learning. The action plan doesn't make that happen, but it gives you the mechanism to allow it to happen. It's not very complicated, so it doesn't take much time, but what it does take is commitment. If you want to use it and make it work for you, it will pay you back many times over.

Extensions

These are a useful way of building up your knowledge and understanding beyond what is contained in Super Series. You don't have to make use of any of them, but if there is a topic that particularly interests you, then this is an excellent way of exploring it further. Extensions include textbooks, videos, computer software, leaflets or similar publications issued by the government or other official bodies, and articles in journals. You will be told how to get hold of such materials, and if you are being supported by a Centre that has a library then you may be able to borrow them there. Don't be afraid to try exploring these sources: they will introduce you to other materials in turn, which you might also want to follow up.

Answers to activities, self-assessments and the quick quiz

These are self-explanatory but, one small but important point: don't look at the answers until you've completed all the questions, and then check back on any where your answer differs from the one given. It may not mean that you've answered it incorrectly – some questions can have a variety of answers, which may be more or less right – but do make sure you know why there is any variation between the one you gave and the one in the workbook.

Here's a summary of the various elements that you have just been reading about. You should have looked at examples of each from your workbook, so that you will be familiar with them; if for any reason you couldn't do this, run through this chapter when you do get your first workbook so that you will understand each main feature before you start.

Workbook introduction

Study links	Links you to other Super Series third edition workbooks
S/NVQ links	Links you to MCI standards
Workbook objectives	Introduces the topic and tells you what you will be able to achieve by the end of the workbook
Activity planner	Points you to those activities that may require some planning

Workbook sessions

Text and graphics	The main topic discussions, case studies and cameos, illustrations and diagrams
Activities and feedback	Confirming your learning
Portfolio activities	Self assessment evidence development exercises
Margin notes	Notes, anecdotes, definitions, quotes and sayings
Extensions	References to further reading and follow-up
Self-assessments	Short end of session test
Summary	Summary of key learning points

Performance checks

Quick quiz	Fifteen short questions covering the whole workbook
Workbook assessment	A case study/simulation exercise
Work-based assignment	A work-based practical exercise linked to S/NVQ and personal competences

Reflect and review

Reflect and review	Review of the original workbook objectives
Action plan	Your personal plan of action
Extensions	Full details of sources of further reading
Answers to activities, self-assessments and the quick quiz	To check your learning

3.3 Getting the most from the workbooks

Hopefully you have now got a good idea of the structure and features of the workbooks. In this section we will run through all the key points and show you how to get the most from them, so that you can learn easily and effectively and, most importantly, turn what you learn into action.

■ *Study links* – help you to plan your learning across a range of workbooks

   ■ Have you used any of these linked workbooks before?
   ■ If so, can you recall the main points? (Re-read the session summaries if necessary.)
   ■ Do you plan to use any of the linked workbooks?
   ■ If so, when; would it be sensible to move directly on to any of them?

- *S/NVQ links* – help you plan and integrate your learning with management standards

    - Are you working towards a S/NVQ?
    - If so, have you read through the linked elements to check out what they cover, particularly in their performance criteria?
    - How competent do you think you are now?
    - How do the element(s) relate to your job?
    - Do you already have any evidence for the element(s)?
    - What evidence do you think you are likely to be able to generate?

- *Workbook objectives* – help you focus on the topic before you start

    - Do you understand what you are expected to be able to do?
    - How much do you currently know in this area?
    - What do you find most challenging in the list of objectives?
    - Have you discussed with your tutor or mentor any concerns that you might have in relation to these objectives?

- *Activity planner* – help you plan ahead, especially for your S/NVQ portfolio

    - What activities in the workbook need to be planned for?
    - How would you undertake them in your workplace?
    - Do you need anybody else's help or agreement?
    - What do you need to do to prepare for the special portfolio activities?

- *Activities* and *work-based assignment* – turning your learning into action, and your actions into evidence of competence

    - Are you willing to undertake them properly and really commit yourself to completing them successfully?
    - Have you completed all the activities?
    - If there were any unexpected outcomes, or problems in undertaking the activities and assignment, do you understand why that was?
    - Do you need any further help or advice in relation to the actions you have taken?

- *Performance checks* and *workbook assessment* – checking out your learning in an applied context

    - Have you fully understood all the concepts in the workbook?
    - Can you apply them in practice?
    - Can you apply them in contexts that you may not be directly familiar with?
    - If you have any problems with the performance checks or the workbook assessment, do you understand why? Have you referred back to the topics and re-read them?
    - Do you need any further help or advice to help you with any problem areas?

- *Reflect and review* – confirming your understanding by fitting it into your existing knowledge and experience

    - Check back to the objectives; have you achieved them all?
    - Does what you have learnt apply easily to your workplace, or have you had to adapt your learning to the specific context of your employer?

21

- Do you know why there are any variations?
- How will you change the way you work as a result of what you have learnt?
- What actions that you have previously undertaken have you had confirmed as being the right way to perform?

■ *Action plan* – putting your learning into action

- Have you defined some clear longer-term goals for yourself?
- Have you established how this workbook will help you move towards the achievement of these goals?
- Have you determined what outcomes you want to achieve as a result of using this workbook?
- Have you planned how to achieve these outcomes (issues, actions, resources and target completion dates)?

3.4 How the audio cassettes are structured

Super Series is a very flexible way of learning. Each workbook is self-contained, but fits together with the others to provide a complete training programme, and they can be used anywhere at any time, allowing you to set the pace and control the process. But they do have one disadvantage – as printed texts they can't completely bring to life the reality of managing a team of people in an office, factory, warehouse, building site or wherever else you might work.

So that's where the audio cassettes come in, because they aren't produced in studios with actors pretending to be managers, but have been recorded in the workplace, using real people talking about real situations. And that means that you can see how so much of the material you will study in Super Series is a direct reflection of the world of work. You can listen to people just like you talking about their jobs and their workteams – how they went about dealing with exactly the same sort of problems as you face, and the sort of solutions they came up with.

There are five audio cassettes, each of which lasts for about 30 minutes and is designed to complement certain specific workbooks, as listed in the table on p. 23.

Each of these cassettes is explained in more detail in Appendix 2, on page 62. You will find it useful to read through these descriptions to help you understand what each is about and see how they can contribute to your learning. You will find that periodically, between the managers talking on the cassettes, there are pauses, flagged up by a brief snatch of music. This may simply be a natural break between topics, but some are followed by questions about the topics being discussed, asking you to reflect on what you have heard and to relate them to your own role. These questions are also reproduced in Appendix 2, for reference, to help you to think about them.

Audio cassette title	Related Super Series workbook title
Reaching Decisions	Making and Taking Decisions Solving Problems
Managing the Bottom Line	Controlling Costs Making a Financial Case Working with Budgets
Customers Count	Caring for the Customer Understanding Quality
Being the Best	Becoming More Effective Delegating Effectively Managing Time Managing Tough Times
Working Together	Leading Your Team Motivating People Working in Teams

In the next section we will look in more detail at how you can get the most from the cassettes, but before you move on to read about that, just spend a little while thinking about the opportunities that you might have to listen to on the cassettes, and how they might increase the outcomes of your programme. Unless you have a disability, you can learn through all your senses; listening to people like you talking about the very real issues that you have to face as a first line manager, and how they deal with them, is one more aid to learning that adds variety and practical examples.

3.5 Getting the most from the cassettes

You don't have to listen to the cassettes at the same time as you use the workbooks, nor do you have to have used all the relevant workbooks to listen to the cassettes – the cassettes are free-standing aids to your learning and understanding of how management operates. You can use them in any way that suits you, in the car on your way to and from work, at home on your stereo system, out walking the dog or jogging with your portable cassette player! It's up to you, as long as you have the opportunity to listen actively to the cassettes and think about what you hear.

What do we mean by 'actively'? Most people listen to audio cassettes in the car, at home or wherever, to hear music, but it is usually music which provides a background to whatever else you are doing. You may be chatting to somebody, thinking about a task to do at work or at home, or where you are going to go on your holiday. That doesn't mean that you aren't listening, but you are only listening with part of your brain, whilst the rest does something else (it's what is called 'multi-tasking' when computers do it). If you want to get the full benefit from the cassettes, you will need to be thinking about what you are hearing, so that you can learn from them.

Each cassette contains a number of specific questions to help you relate its contents to your own workplace, but there are some broader points which you might also want to consider, to help you fit these real-life case studies to your learning from the Super Series workbooks. To help you, here are some questions you might want to think about as you listen to each one:

a *What do I already know about this aspect of management?*	We learn by adding to what we know already, so it's useful to reflect on your existing knowledge and behaviour when trying to understand anything new. Think about this question before you start listening, to prepare yourself to learn.
b *How do the participants' descriptions of their working practices compare to mine?*	Not every manager behaves in the same way, nor should they. You have to adapt any principle to your own workplace, your team and your own personality. So it's useful to make comparisons between the situations described and your own, to understand what you do the same, what you do differently, and why. The cassettes aren't meant to be the best or only practice, just to describe real-life management in action. The important question for you is not just 'What would I have done?' but 'Why would I do it that way?'.
c *What principles of management that I know about are illustrated by the participants?*	Can you explain why managers do things the way they do? Is it because that was how they were managed themselves, or that's the only way they know how to do it, or is it because they understand some important principles of management, such as you will learn through Super Series, and make conscious decisions to perform effectively?
d *What can I learn about my own behaviour and how to develop myself from what I have heard?*	Learning depends on understanding, making sense of what you've read, heard or seen and fitting it into what you already know in such a way that you can use it effectively. Listen to these cassettes and reflect on what you've heard, and then make a conscious decision to use what you have learnt in your work role.

Different people will find that they can use the cassettes in different ways, according to their particular learning style. Each person must choose what suits them, but here is a suggestion about how you can get the most from the audio cassettes:

- Ask yourself the first question (*What do I already know about this aspect of management?*) to prepare for the first playing.
- Play the first section of the cassette through once, to the first set of questions, just listening to the people talking and making sure that you can hear them clearly. This will give you a chance to get used to the voices and accents, and to get an idea of what they are talking about.
- Play the section through again, and answer the questions posed about the topic covered; repeat this for each section. You might find it useful to make some notes if you have the opportunity, although if you are playing the cassette in the car this may not be possible straight away. Repeat this for the remaining sections.
- When you have listened to the whole cassette, and answered the specific questions posed at the end of each section, look at the rest of the broader questions above (b–d) and try to answer them as carefully as possible. (Your Centre may choose to organize this activity as a part of a workshop session, and you might have the opportunity to discuss your thoughts with your group.)
- Is there any way that you can put the ideas and practices you have heard about on the cassette into practice? Think about your answer to the last question carefully, and use the opportunity presented by the cassettes to help you to develop your own managerial performance.

To support you in doing this, there is a simple action plan over the page which you might want to use to get the most from each of the audio cassettes.

Getting the most from the audio cassettes: action plan

Before you start listening:

What do I already know about this aspect of management?

During the cassette:

How do the participants' descriptions of their working practices compare to mine? What would I have done in the situations described, and why?

What principles of management that I know about are illustrated by the participants?

After listening to the complete cassette:

What can I learn about my own behaviour and how to develop myself from what I have heard?

What will I do now as a result of listening to the cassette?

4 Routes to capability and competence

You have now learned quite a lot about the Super Series materials:

■ what they contain
■ how they are structured
■ the distinctive features of the workbooks and audio cassette tapes
■ how you can use these features to help you to learn.

You now need to think about what you can achieve by using them, especially any qualifications that you may wish to work towards. This chapter of the *User Guide* explains how you can use Super Series material to help you achieve one of the internationally recognized NEBS Management qualifications.

It is useful to think of Super Series as being about *learning* and qualifications as being about the outcome of the assessment of that learning. You are likely to be far more successful in your learning if you consider how you are going to be assessed when you set off to learn. Why? Because different qualifications require different assessments in different areas of learning.

To help you understand how you will be assessed and how your learning will be affected, it is helpful to look at two different approaches, one that assesses *capability* and one that assesses *competence*. But first, what do these two words mean?

Capability is:

Possessing the knowledge and skills required to perform a task effectively

and competence is:

The ability to perform in work roles or jobs to the standard required in employment

What's the difference? Well, capability awards focus their assessment on the possession of knowledge and skills which indicate that you are capable of performing the role effectively, whereas competence awards focus assessment on your actual performance in the job.

The difference is significant, since the types of assessment are quite distinct and different people will find that they prefer one form of assessment to another. That's why NEBS Management offers awards which feature both systems of assessment, those that look for capability – you have shown that you *could* fulfil the requirements made of a supervisor, team leader or first line manager – and competence – you have shown under your normal working conditions that you *can* fulfil those requirements.

The rest of this *User Guide* shows you just what is involved in both types of qualification and how the workbooks and audio cassettes can help you develop both your capability and your competence.

4.2 Learning methods

You can use Super Series material as a major part of your learning for both types of award route qualifications using any one (or a combination) of these flexible learning methods:

- Distance learning
- Open/flexible learning
- Mixed mode
- Customized

What are these different methods and what do they mean for you?

Distance learning

This is offered mainly by specialist Distance Learning Centres and relies almost entirely on the use of the workbooks and tapes and, possibly, some of the Centre's own material, as there will be no group or workshop activities with a tutor. Support and assessment is conducted by correspondence (or more likely today, e-mail or the Internet) or by telephone.

Distance learning is particularly useful for those who live overseas, have difficulty getting to a training and support centre (if you live or work in very rural areas or on drilling rigs, for example), have mobility problems (a physical disability or poor access to transport, perhaps) or have a job that is particularly demanding or unusual (irregular shifts, maybe).

Open/flexible learning

This study route will have some distance learning features in as far as it will use Super Series material to deliver the self-study component of the course, which you will undertake at home or at work, but there will also be a significant number of attended group workshops run at a Centre by a qualified tutor.

There are many different open/flexible learning (OFL) models that you could be offered even against a standard national award programme (different Centres use different models) which is beneficial as this gives variety and choice. OFL programmes are also characterized by all year round enrolment, special start-up induction sessions (you could be working through this *User Guide* with a tutor as part of just such a session) and workshop activities that use case studies, role plays and business simulation to help apply the newly acquired self-study input.

Mixed mode

Yet another variation on the routes to study is mixed mode. In many ways this resembles OFL in as far as there will always be a self-study component (though significantly reduced) and group sessions and workshops. However, it is not unusual to find a more conventional mix of learning styles such as formal lectures, seminars and tutorials that offer the benefits of working together with others as well as the benefits of flexibility.

Many Centres, especially the in-company ones, use the mixed mode approach as an ideal opportunity to bring in specialist internal and external speakers.

Customized

Some organizations have very specific requirements for the development of their supervisors/first line managers and at the same time wish to offer them the opportunity to achieve a nationally recognized qualification. Super Series material is used within a unique, tailored programme which is often delivered in a way similar to the mixed mode route but which also utilizes even more innovative and less conventional combinations of resources for its delivery. An example would be a residential leadership/survival programme conducted in a remote location.

4.3 Capability awards

NEBS Management – the National Examining Board for Supervision and Management – is part of City and Guilds, over thirty years old and currently the largest awarding body for management qualifications in the UK, with over 1000 Centres and around 40 000 student registrations every year. The Centres range from Universities to individual employers, although the majority are Colleges of Further Education. The Centres also include both large and small private training companies and voluntary organizations, and all branches of the armed forces. Centres exist throughout the UK and Ireland, and in the Middle East, Africa, Asia, Australasia and Eastern and Western Europe.

NEBS Management offers two first-level capability awards – the *NEBS Management Introductory Award* and the *NEBS Management Certificate*. There are two other capability awards available at a higher level that you may want to progress to on completion of your current programme – the *NEBS Management Introductory Diploma* and the *NEBS Management Diploma*.

The NEBS Management Introductory Award

This programme is a minimum of thirty hours, must be completed in one year and is open to all practising and potential supervisors and managers who wish to take a first step in formal management development.

Programmes that are based on flexible learning will include an induction/ briefing session, an agreed period of self-study and a six-hour skills development workshop, or approved alternative. Self-study means satisfactory completion of at least five Super Series workbooks, one from each of the four workbook groups (Managing Activities, Managing Resources, Managing People and Managing Information) plus a fifth from any group. Assessment usually includes submission and assessment of some written work such as one or more work-based assignment or completion of some other approved task.

There are several approved alternatives to the basic route described above, which change the mix between self-study, the number of workbooks and workshops and the form of assessment. Your local NEBS Management Centre will have the details.

The NEBS Management Certificate

This is the best known NEBS Management qualification and consists of four main *modules*:

- Managing Human Resources
- Managing Products and Services
- Managing Information
- Managing Financial Resources

Each of these modules is divided into detailed topic areas (or modules) as shown on the following page.

Managing Human Resources

1 Managing People as Individuals
2 Managing People as Members of Groups and Teams
3 Recruitment and Selection
4 Assessing, Training and Developing Individuals
5 Managing Work
6 Employee Relations
7 Managing Health and Safety of Workteam

Managing Products and Services

1 Quality of Products and Services
2 Techniques of Planning, Organizing and Controlling Work
3 Raw Materials, Supplies and Equipment
4 Health and Safety
5 The Environment

Managing Information

1 Collection of Information
2 Storage and Retrieval of Information
3 Use of Information
4 General Communication Skills
5 Oral Communication
6 Written Communication

Managing Financial Resources

1 The National and International Context
2 Finance within the Organization
3 Cost Control within the Organization
4 Budgetary Control and Performance

You will probably have noticed how close these titles are to the new Super Series, which shouldn't come as a surprise as they have been developed very much in parallel.

This programme is a minimum of 240 hours, must be completed in three years (in practice the average time is 9–12 months) and is open to all practising and potential supervisors and managers who wish to further develop their formal management skills. It is of particular value as a follow-on programme to the Introductory Award.

Programmes that are based on flexible learning or mixed mode routes will include an induction/briefing session, an agreed period of self-study, mandatory attendance at skills development workshops and satisfactory completion of various assessments. Self-study means completion of a maximum of twenty-three Super Series workbooks (selected under guidance from the four workbook areas) plus the title *Project and Report Writing* in certain circumstances. The five workshops will each be six hours long and designed to help you apply your learning and develop skills alongside other course members. The table on page 33 will help you decide which workbooks to use for each of the four modules.

Assessment will include satisfactory completion of four specially designed written assignments, a 3000-word problem-solving project, a case study exercise, and a one-to-one interview with a NEBS Management external verifier. The workbook assessments and work-based assignments from your workbooks may be used as part of this assessment – your tutor or trainer will explain this to you.

As we have already mentioned, the Super Series workbooks are designed to support these modules, and in the table opposite you can see that each workbook is mapped against the appropriate module titles for which it is relevant. The fact that the Certificate consists of four distinct modules allows you to decide to work towards the whole award as part of a single programme (an *integrated* programme) or module by module (a *modular* programme). This choice is to enable you to plan a programme which suits your particular needs and goals. Your Centre will help you to decide which suits you.

Super Series workbooks and NEBS Management Certificate modules

Column groups — **Managing Human Resources**: Managing People as Individuals; Managing People as Members of Groups and Teams; Recruitment and Selection; Assessing, Training and Developing Individuals; Managing Work; Employee Relations; Managing Health and Safety of Workteam. **Managing Products and Services**: Quality of Products and Services; Techniques of Planning, Organizing and Controlling Work; Raw Materials, Supplies and Equipment; Health and Safety; The Environment. **Managing Information**: Collection of Information; Storage and Retrieval of Information; Use of Information; General Communication Skills; Oral Communication; Written Communication. **Managing Financial Resources**: The National and International Context; Finance within the Organization; Cost Control within the Organization; Budgetary Control and Performance.

NEBS Management Block	Managing People as Individuals	Managing People as Members of Groups and Teams	Recruitment and Selection	Assessing, Training and Developing Individuals	Managing Work	Employee Relations	Managing Health and Safety of Workteam	Quality of Products and Services	Techniques of Planning, Organizing and Controlling Work	Raw Materials, Supplies and Equipment	Health and Safety	The Environment	Collection of Information	Storage and Retrieval of Information	Use of Information	General Communication Skills	Oral Communication	Written Communication	The National and International Context	Finance within the Organization	Cost Control within the Organization	Budgetary Control and Performance
A Managing Activities																						
1 Planning and Controlling Work									●													
2 Understanding Quality								●														
3 Achieving Quality								●														
4 Caring for the Customer								●														
5 Marketing and Selling																				●		
6 Managing a Safe Environment							●				●	●										
7 Managing Lawfully – Health, Safety and Environment							●				●	●										
8 Preventing Accidents							●				●	●										
9 Leading Change	●	●																				
B Managing Resources																						
1 Controlling Physical Resources										●												
2 Improving Efficiency								●	●													
3 Understanding Finance																			●	●		
4 Working with Budgets																						●
5 Controlling Costs																					●	
6 Making a Financial Case				●																●	●	
C Managing People																						
1 How Organizations Work									●													
2 Managing with Authority	●	●																				
3 Leading Your Team		●																				
4 Delegatng Effectively	●	●																				
5 Working in Teams		●																				
6 Motivating People	●	●																				
7 Securing the Right People			●																			
8 Appraising Performance				●																		
9 Planning Training and Development				●																		
10 Delivering Training				●																		
11 Managing Lawfully – People and Employment						●																
12 Commitment to Equality						●																
13 Becoming More Effective	●	●																				
14 Managing Tough Times	●	●																				
15 Managing Time																						
D Managing Information																						
1 Collecting Information													●									
2 Storing and Retrieving Information														●								
3 Information in Management															●							
4 Communication in Management																●	●					
5 Listening and Speaking																●	●					
6 Communicating in Groups																●	●					
7 Writing Effectively																		●				
8 Project and Report Writing				●														●				
9 Making and Taking Decisions				●					●					●								
10 Solving Problems									●					●								

4.4 Competence awards

Competence is defined as:

The ability to perform in work roles or jobs to the standard required in employment

In other words, competence is about 'performance', not just 'knowing how to perform'. But of course, if you don't know how to perform, then you won't be able to perform. That's why S/NVQs must assess both

- your performance (can you do it?)
- your 'underpinning knowledge and understanding' (do you know how, when and why to do it?).

The NEBS Management S/NVQs are designed to assess your competence – to determine whether or not you can perform in the way described in the standards. They recognize that:

- you can develop your competence in the workplace just as effectively as through formal education and training;
- what education and training you do have should be based on what supervisors and first line managers actually do.

This is where Super Series can help, by enabling your Centre to put together a flexible programme which fits your personal development needs.

You may well have already learnt a lot about Health and Safety and recruiting new staff. Why should you go on a course to learn what you are already quite competent in doing? You also know a lot about quality control systems, although you would like to learn a bit more, particularly about team problem solving. By using Super Series workbooks, your employer, college or training centre can put together a package of training that suits you personally.

The map opposite shows you how the various standards in the S/NVQs match against the workbooks in Super Series. This can help (with the assistance of your tutor or training adviser) to pick those which will be most useful to you in developing your knowledge and skills and becoming competent.

Super Series workbooks and Level 3 standards: Map

Mandatory units: A1, B1, C1, C4, D1 (elements A1.1–D1.3). Optional units: C7, C9, C12, C15, E6, E8, F5, F7 (elements C7.1–F7.2).

Workbooks	A1.1	A1.2	A1.3	B1.1	B1.2	C1.1	C1.2	C4.1	C4.2	C4.3	D1.1	D1.2	D1.3	C7.1	C7.2	C9.1	C9.2	C9.3	C9.4	C12.1	C12.2	C12.3	C15.1	C15.2	E6.1	E6.2	E8.1	E8.2	E8.3	F5.1	F5.2	F5.3	F5.4	F7.1	F7.2
A Managing Activities																																			
1 Planning and Controlling Work	●		●			●														●															
2 Understanding Quality	●	●	●																											●	●				
3 Achieving Quality	●		●																	●												●	●		
4 Caring for the Customer			●					●		●																									
5 Marketing and Selling			●								●																								
6 Managing a Safe Environment		●				●																													
7 Managing Lawfully – Health, Safety and Environment	●																																		
8 Preventing Accidents	●										●	●																							
9 Leading Change		●														●		●																	
B Managing Resources																																			
1 Controlling Physical Resources					●																														
2 Improving Efficiency				●	●																														
3 Understanding Finance				●	●						●	●																							
4 Working with Budgets				●	●						●	●																							
5 Controlling Costs				●	●																														
6 Making a Financial Case		●	●									●																							
C Managing People																																			
1 How Organizations Work		●	●						●																										
2 Managing with Authority						●		●		●													●												
3 Leading Your Team						●														●	●	●													
4 Delegating Effectively																				●	●	●													
5 Working in Teams								●		●										●	●	●													
6 Motivating People														●	●		●				●														
7 Securing the Right People														●	●																				
8 Appraising Performance						●	●													●	●														
9 Planning Training and Development														●		●																			
10 Delivering Training														●	●	●	●			●	●	●													
11 Managing Lawfully – People and Employment																								●											
12 Commitment to Equality		●						●																											
13 Becoming More Effective						●	●																												
14 Managing Tough Times		●																					●												
15 Managing Time						●	●																												
D Managing Information																																			
1 Collecting Information							●					●	●																						
2 Storing and Retrieving Information	●	●				●					●	●																							
3 Information in Management							●		●		●	●								●															
4 Communication in Management									●		●	●																							
5 Listening and Speaking	●					●		●		●	●	●			●																				
6 Communicating in Groups						●	●		●		●	●								●												●			
7 Writing Effectively			●								●	●																							
8 Project and Report Writing											●	●																							
9 Making and Taking Decisions						●					●																								
10 Solving Problems			●			●					●	●																							

Two additional points to note about the S/NVQ standards:

■ There are different S/NVQs for different levels of managerial performance, and Super Series can be used for Level 3 and some parts of the Level 4 qualifications. Your tutor or training adviser will help you work out which is appropriate r you.

■ The standards we have been talking about up to now are what are called *functional standards* – the standards that describe the particular performance required by managers at different levels in relation to particular types of tasks.

There are also some standards which relate to more general types of performance, called *personal competence*. Again, your Centre will tell you more about these, but the workbooks in Super Series can also help you to develop these, and you will see from the 'map' opposite which ones are useful for particular areas of personal competence.

Super Series workbooks and personal competence: Map

Workbooks:	Acting assertively	Acting strategically	Behaving ethically	Building teams	Communicating	Focusing on results	Influencing others	Managing self	Searching for information	Thinking and taking decisions
A Managing Activities										
1 Planning and Controlling Work						●				
2 Understanding Quality						●				
3 Achieving Quality						●				
4 Caring for the Customer						●				
5 Marketing and Selling						●				
6 Managing a Safe Environment			●							
7 Managing Lawfully – Health, Safety and Environment			●							
8 Preventing Accidents			●							
9 Leading Change						●	●			
B Managing Resources										
1 Controlling Physical Resources						●				
2 Improving Efficiency						●				
3 Understanding Finance		●				●				
4 Working with Budgets		●				●				
5 Controlling Costs		●				●				
6 Making a Financial Case							●			
C Managing People										
1 How Organizations Work				●		●				
2 Managing with Authority				●			●			
3 Leading Your Team				●						
4 Delegatng Effectively				●			●			
5 Working in Teams				●						
6 Motivating People				●			●			
7 Securing the Right People			●	●						
8 Appraising Performance			●	●	●	●				
9 Planning Training and Development				●				●		
10 Delivering Training				●	●		●			
11 Managing Lawfully – People and Employment			●							
12 Commitment to Equality			●							
13 Becoming More Effective	●							●		
14 Managing Tough Times	●		●			●	●	●		
15 Managing Time	●					●				
D Managing Information										
1 Collecting Information									●	
2 Storing and Retrieving Information									●	
3 Information in Management					●				●	
4 Communication in Management					●	●				
5 Listening and Speaking					●					
6 Communicating in Groups					●			●		
7 Writing Effectively					●			●		
8 Project and Report Writing					●			●		
9 Making and Taking Decisions	●					●				●
10 Solving Problems	●				●	●				●

Competence awards assessment

Competence awards are part of a national structure:

Country	Overseen by	Called
England Wales Northern Ireland	Qualifications and Curriculum Authority (QCA)	National Vocational Qualifications (NVQs)
Scotland	Scottish Qualifications Authority (SQA)	Scottish Vocational Qualifications (SVQs)

The NEBS Management S/NVQs are part of this structure, using standards of performance which were developed by a body called the Management Charter Initiative (MCI). They offer supervisors and first line managers an opportunity to develop their practical competence in the workplace to national standards and to have this competence recognized with a national qualification.

You will see from the S/NVQ map on the previous page that the S/NVQs are broken down into *units* and *elements*. Some of these units are:

- *mandatory* (you must demonstrate your competence in these)

and some are

- *optional* (you need to be competent in some of these areas, depending on your particular role).

You will be assessed against each element of a unit, and once you have been assessed as competent you can ask for it to be credited, offering you flexibility in your assessment to match the flexibility offered by Super Series.

NEBS Management will issue a certificate which shows that you have been credited with a particular unit, helping you to build up the full S/NVQ in your own time and allowing you to take breaks if you need to (for example, through job changes or periods away from paid employment).

Because S/NVQs require you to demonstrate competent performance, in order for you to join a programme you must:

- have access to a workplace now, or expect to have such access in the future, or have had recent experience which you can use to enable you to produce evidence;
- be or have been in a work role which enables you to demonstrate your competence at the appropriate level and across the range of tasks required by the award.

If you are currently employed, this should not be a problem; if not, your Centre will probably be able to arrange for you to gain some practical experience and also show how you can use evidence of past experience. Your Centre will ask you to undertake some form of initial diagnosis, to identify where you are currently competent. This could be text-based or computer-based and the process might be called *Assessment of Prior Learning* (APL) (or *Assessment of Prior Experience*, APE) and can include relevant unpaid work as well as paid (for example, work with a charity or voluntary group). One of the outcomes of such a process is that not only does it show where you are currently competent, it also shows you where you are not yet competent, and can help identify any underpinning knowledge gaps which could be closed by using Super Series workbooks – especially the special *portfolio activities* and *work-based assignments* which may be able to provide acceptable competence evidence.

If your local Centre is approved to offer S/NVQ awards they should be able to match this with a wide range of support including:

- Advice and guidance on the appropriate assessment route to follow.
- Initial assessment or audit of competence to enable any prior learning to be accredited.
- Preparation of a personal development plan to help you organize your study programme.
- Guidance on developing a portfolio of evidence for assessment of competence.
- Support for your learning, through the provision of suitable learning material and workshops to practise and develop your competence.
- Assessment and verification, leading to unit accreditation and the award of your S/NVQ.

5 Managing your learning

5.1 Introduction

One of the Personal Competences we all have to develop is managing ourselves. In the earlier parts of this guide we have:

- given you an overview of the new Super Series edition;
- explained what each workbook and audio cassette contains;
- described the structure and features of the workbooks and audio cassettes;
- introduced you to the capability and competence routes to NEBS Management qualifications.

In this chapter we will look at how you can manage your own learning effectively and get the maximum benefit from the time and the effort you will be spending on your management development.

We will begin by looking again at the idea of flexible learning, see some of the drawbacks (because nothing is perfect) and show you how to overcome these. This study advice is designed to help you get the best out of your Super Series workbooks, both in the way you organize your work and in the way you undertake it.

This is helped by proper planning, setting aside fixed times and undertaking fixed tasks according to a timetable which will give you the main prerequisite for flexible learning – self-discipline! That doesn't mean that you are on your own. Your Centre can be a valuable source of advice and support, and you will be encouraged to use this to make your learning as straightforward and as effective as possible.

You have already learnt about the action plan, and how that can help you translate your learning into action. You will also be encouraged to identify some broader aims for your learning and your career, so that you have a clear idea where you expect the course you are embarking on to lead you. As we have said, it is not possible to plan in detail for longer periods of time, but that doesn't stop you giving your learning and your work some direction so that your specific, shorter-term goals build up into a coherent development programme.

40

5.2 Flexible learning

Flexible learning is a term you may not have been familiar with before starting this programme or reading this *User Guide*. You may have heard of 'open learning' or 'distance learning' and wonder if they are the same thing, or if not, what the difference is.

In practice, different people and organizations use these labels in slightly different ways, so here is what we mean by flexible learning:

Flexible learning means that learners can negotiate their programme so that they can work at times and locations appropriate to their needs, priorities and opportunities, to suit their existing learning and experiences and to meet particular objectives

In other words, a flexible learning programme will take account of:

- what you already know and can do;
- what you want to know and be able to do in the future;
- when you are able to learn and when you want to start and finish;
- where you want to learn;
- how you want to learn.

This in turn means having a variety of resources available to help you learn, such as:

- audio and video equipment;
- interactive IT equipment;
- textbooks and journals;
- learning materials such as Super Series.

It will also include:

- people (such as tutors, trainers, mentors, etc.);
- facilities (seminar rooms or training rooms, learning resource centres, etc.) where you can meet and access these resources.

Super Series enables Centres to operate flexibly. The approval of Centres by NEBS Management ensures that when Centres use materials like Super Series they have the infrastructure (the resources and the organization) to use them effectively, so that they can offer you the quality of support you need. Not all Centres function in the same way, because each Centre will be meeting different needs and operating within a different environment, but the combination of Super Series and NEBS Management means that if a Centre says it can do something, you can feel confident that it can!

5.3 Learning to learn

We all spend our time learning. From our first breath we have to be able to learn from the range of experiences we are exposed to, and as managers we are always expected to deal with the new and the unexpected. This means learning all the time.

But flexible learning demands particular learning skills, which you may not have used that often or which need improving. This section of the *User Guide* will help you identify and work on them, so that you can use the Super Series workbooks effectively.

There are three main types of skill you need to focus on:

- Using your time effectively
- Using your resources effectively
- Using your ability to learn effectively

Using your time effectively

Time is the most precious resource we have. It:

- is limited in its availability,
- must be spent,
- can't be used again!

You have to look after it carefully and spend it wisely, so that you get the most out of what is available. With flexible learning there are no set times when you must attend classes or training sessions to provide a disciplined environment – both of which take some responsibility from you.

Flexible learning is 'learner centred'; that is, the time and place of your sessions are up to you, though you may need to get the agreement of others, such as your employer or your family. The trouble is, it is easy to put off or avoid them if something crops up, in a way that you wouldn't if you were attending regular classes. One solution is to put aside a regular time to work in, and treat it as if it were a regular class.

If your employer is prepared to make some time during working hours for you to study, this can be agreed with your line manager and workteam. It should then be treated as a fixed period when you are working. If you are using your own time, then do the same thing, but agree with your family and friends that this is 'Super Series time' – time when you aren't available, except in emergencies.

How much time? Well, the whole point of flexible learning is that you use the amount of time that *you* need, so the total length can vary (although the workbooks are designed to take about 8–10 hours each). How you break that down into sessions must suit you, but try to avoid doing it all in one sitting, making it a chore and reducing what you get out of a workbook. Alternatively, sessions of less than one hour are probably too short, except to conclude a workbook session, perhaps answering the self-assessment questions.

You will find that you will get the most out of Super Series if you organize your learning around fixed periods of between one and three hours, with a short break in the middle, to give yourself a rest. We also suggest that you aim to complete a workbook in about two weeks, so two periods a week of about 2–2½ hours each should enable you to keep to this sort of schedule.

Using your resources effectively

In addition to the workbooks and audio materials and suitable playback equipment, you will need:

■ a notebook and pen or pencil,
■ a calculator (for some workbooks),
■ somewhere quiet to work, and
■ your commitment.

The workbooks will be supplied by the Centre. You should be able to find the writing materials and calculator somewhere, but the commitment must come from you! What you will find is that once you get started, particularly if you work at a regular time and pace, the commitment will build up and carry you through. One of the most rewarding things about the Super Series is completing the workbooks at regular intervals, giving you a real sense of achievement.

By the way, why do you need a notebook and pen? You can make notes in the workbooks, as the margins are deliberately made wide enough for you to do so, and the summaries at the end of each session give you the essential points of each workbook. But a notebook can be useful for:

■ rough working of answers to activities,
■ making notes of 'things to do', and
■ writing your own summaries, which some people find a real help in learning something new.

What you *don't want* is a telephone, visitors, other people working or playing round you, or the TV playing, although some people find that music is a good background. If you can't achieve this in the office or at home, then if your employer or the Centre has a learning resource centre or study room/library, try to use that at fixed times. You should also try your local public library which will probably have a reference area which is quiet and warm, and has the right environment for you to learn in, and which might itself be an open learning centre. If the only place you can work in is the bedroom, then try to get a desk and upright chair of some sort to use. Lying across the bed is not advised!

Using your ability to learn effectively

We have already stressed that your personal commitment is the major resource that you bring with you, but commitment alone is not enough. You will need some specific learning skills to carry you through (not particularly difficult skills for most people, but significant ones nevertheless).

Do you have any difficulties with reading? For example:

■ Do you have a disability (perhaps problems with your sight, or perhaps you suffer from dyslexia)?
■ Have your reading skills been fully developed?
■ Is English, perhaps, not your first language?

If so, tell your tutor, trainer or other learning adviser. They should be able to give you advice on how to overcome such problems, ranging from aids to overcome physical disabilities, to specialist support services to overcome learning difficulties.

However, reading skills aren't enough on their own. What you also need is the ability to read and make sense of what you are reading. Super Series helps you do this by asking you questions at intervals throughout the text, questions to test that you have understood something and questions to get you to work things out for yourself. Answer these questions seriously, because they are there for a purpose. An ordinary textbook just presents information without any interaction with the reader, asking you to do no more than read it.

Learning resources like the Super Series workbooks help you:

■ to think,
■ to calculate,
■ to ask others,
■ to explore,
■ to analyse,
■ to compare,
■ to measure

– in other words, to learn!

This is supported by the summaries which recap what you have learnt (so that you can see your progress) but also enable you to refer back to them. This is particularly useful when you are starting a new session and it has been a few days since you finished the previous session; re-reading the summary can get you back up to speed so that you start the new session with confidence at the point you left off with the last one.

5.4 Planning your learning

We have already talked about two important aspects of planning, your action plan and the need to set aside specific time for working on Super Series. In this section we want to encourage you to use the action plan to support your learning and to link that into your daily and weekly activities.

One way of helping you to keep to a schedule for the completion of Super Series and the achievement of your goal (a NEBS Management Certificate or S/NVQ 3, say) is to draw up a study plan. Your Centre may well have a particular model for you to use, but if not, here is an example of what we mean by a study plan which you can draw up and use yourself. It is in two parts; the first is designed to give you an overall plan for the whole programme, with targets for the completion of workbooks, and the order in which you intend completing them:

Study plan I		
Month	**Workbook**	**Completed**
March	How Organizations Work	✓
	Working in Teams	✓
April	Leading Your Team	✓
	Delegating Effectively	
May	Understanding Quality	
	Achieving Quality	
June	Planning Training and Development	
	Delivering Training	
July	Planning and Controlling Work	
	Holiday	
August	Holiday	
	Information in Management	
September	Project and Report Writing	
	Marketing and Selling	
October	Controlling Physical Resources	
	Understanding Finance	
November	Working with Budgets	
	Controlling Costs	
December	Project	
	Christmas	
January	Presentation	

The second is a shorter-term, more detailed plan for completing each workbook:

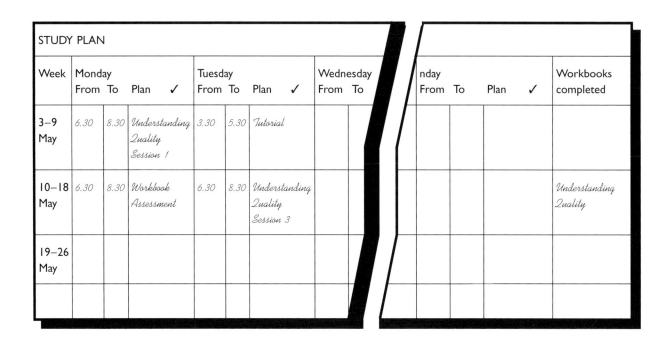

STUDY PLAN																	
Week	Monday				Tuesday				Wednesday			nday					Workbooks
	From	To	Plan	✓	From	To	Plan	✓	From	To		From	To	Plan	✓		completed
3–9 May	6.30	8.30	Understanding Quality Session 1		3.30	5.30	Tutorial										
10–18 May	6.30	8.30	Workbook Assessment		6.30	8.30	Understanding Quality Session 3										Understanding Quality
19–26 May																	

This particular learner has just completed *Understanding Quality* and is moving on to *Achieving Quality*. Writing down the name of each workbook as it is completed is a useful reminder of how much you have achieved, but only planning in detail for about two or three workbooks at a time will stop you getting hopelessly out of step if you miss a couple of sessions or get a little bit behind in completing them. This learner has also planned in a tutorial. In Chapter 6 of the *User Guide* we will tell you how to get the most from such support.

5.5 Your personal development plan

Super Series is not an end in itself, but a means to an end, and a set of stepping stones to guide you towards your career goal. The study plan will help you organize your time, to follow those stepping stones, but that's all it is designed to do, to be used as a planning and monitoring device to help you manage your progress. Each workbook also has an action plan at the end, which is designed to help you put your learning into action, and these are far more critical to your overall career progression, since learning about supervisory management and performing competently in the role are two very different things.

As we have said, the action plan at the end of each workbook is designed to help you put your learning into practice and to perfect the skills you will be acquiring, and it will also help you to develop your portfolio of evidence if you are aiming for a S/NVQ. By consciously planning how you are going to put your learning into action, you will be able to combine them into a personal development plan (PDP). The PDP isn't just a series of individual action plans though; it is much more than that. A PDP is a way of putting what you learn and how you apply that learning into the broader context of your personal and career goals, and of identifying and taking advantage of all the opportunities and the support services available to you.

This could be done in several ways, but your Centre may well ask you to undertake quite a substantial exercise to help you identify where you are now and where you want to get to over the medium to long term (that is, the next year to five years). This could comprise:

■ initial assessment (individual or team tests and exercises, self, peer and line manager assessment);
■ career evaluation;
■ job role analysis;
■ various personality inventories, team inventories, etc.;
■ learning styles assessment;
■ a goal setting exercise.

These sorts of activities are designed to answer three questions:

■ Where are you now?
■ Where do you want to be?
■ How can you get there?

Such exercises will, at the very least, help you and your tutors/trainers work out the best route for you in your learning programme and can, at the very most, provide you with the opportunity to take major decisions about your future and how you want to take some control of it.

The PDP and the individual action plans in each workbook are the mechanism for doing this, and the outcomes of any initial exercises and the goals that you agree for your future personal development provide the framework within which to set out on the Super Series workbooks.

6 Help and support

6.1 Introduction

We have mentioned several times how important it is to take advantage of the various support services available to you, to ensure that you get the most out of your programme and achieve the goals that you have set for yourself. In this chapter of the *User Guide* we will help you to do this.

This includes using the support available from your Centre and employer, from the various external sources (including friends and family), and from NEBS Management itself. Finally we will ask you some questions to help you think about where you might want to go after you have competed this programme.

6.2 Using internal support

There are a range of different people with various different roles who may be available to help you; you should check out just who is available for you and make sure that you take full advantage of their support when you need it.

Tutors/trainers/instructors

Your Centre may be your employer, a university or college, or an independent training provider. Whichever it is, there will be someone who has the task of managing your programme and supervising your learning. They may not be the same person, as the course may be organized by one person and you may be teamed up with someone else as tutor or supervisor. It is important to be clear what the difference in roles is, so that you can be sure that you get the maximum benefit from either. (Of course, if one person is doing both jobs, the following role descriptions apply to that one person.)

The programme organizer will be responsible for liaising with NEBS Management and possibly with your employer or line manager, will handle all the paperwork and the maintenance of records, and may supply you with your copies of Super Series. The tutor/adviser/supervisor will monitor your progress and be available (perhaps at particular times) for you to turn to for advice, for the answer to questions, and possibly for assessment; if you are embarking on a S/NVQ, this person will be the one who gives you advice on the creation of your portfolio.

This support might be available on a drop-in basis, but it might be structured as regular sessions or as a telephone advice line at particular times. Make sure you know when the support is available, and whether it is only available at certain times or as a service on demand.

Mentor

The role of a mentor is to help make a link between the workplace, your learning and your assessment, so that you can develop your performance and demonstrate your competence as effectively as possible, given the opportunities available. To do this, mentors will need to be:

- familiar with your programme and the Super Series workbooks;
- accessible to you at times that match your needs;
- willing to provide you with advice, guidance and support;
- informed about your workplace and your role in it.

Your mentor could be your line manager or another manager in your employing organization, or a member of the Centre's training staff. The main advantage of your manager being your mentor is that a manager may be in the best position to advise you on:

- the development opportunities available to you in the workplace (for example, projects or placements);
- gaining access to workplace activities where competence can be developed and demonstrated for assessment purposes;
- the way that your workplace performance is developing;
- how best to gather evidence for assessment.

Training staff acting as mentors may not always be quite as well placed to help you in the workplace but they should be able to advise you on how best to:

- make use of development opportunities that you or they know to be available;
- respond to workplace situations which offer the potential for developing and demonstrating competence;
- transfer learning from the training situation to the workplace.

Learning Resource Centres

We have already mentioned, several times, that there may well be some sort of Learning Resource Centre available to you; it could be called that, or any of the following terms:

- Open Learning Centre
- Drop-In Centre or Workshop
- Study Centre
- Library (which may also be an Open Learning Centre)

Its name doesn't matter; what does matter is what is available and how well you use it. Don't be afraid to go in and ask the staff for advice on what is available and how to gain access to it, particularly if the Centre doesn't arrange some sort of induction session for you. You may well find that the Centre has a number of personal computers (PCs) available for you. These can be particularly useful if you are producing assignments or projects. If you don't know how to use a PC, you will probably find that it's possible to learn the basics in the Centre, a skill which will always be useful, no matter what else you do.

Colleagues, managers and specialist staff

Samuel Johnson, who compiled the first English dictionary said:

'There are two kinds of knowledge, you know something or you know where to find out about it.'

Knowing who can help you is a sign that you can recognize your own need for help, and that you can identify the best source of help available. It is not a sign of weakness that you ask for help, but a sign of sensible managerial ability.

Your workplace is full of people who can help; in most cases all you've got to do is to ask them. Colleagues – other supervisors/first line managers, and members of your workteam – all have skills and knowledge that you can draw on. Senior managers and other specialist staff can be useful; everybody likes to be recognized for their abilities and skills, and going to people and asking them to give you help when they have the time to do so can often be quite a compliment to them.

Other trainees

You may be working on your own, but it is likely that you are part of a group all working towards the same qualification. If so, your fellow trainees can also be a really useful resource for each other. By discussing issues, giving examples from their own employer or experiences, and by revealing the same problems that you might have had, the group can jointly support its members.

Your Centre may encourage this by the use of *Action Learning Sets* (or something with a similar type of name), grouping you and others together and encouraging you to plan your learning and assessment jointly. Even without this formal arrangement, you will be able to work together if you are willing to make the effort, and you will find that it takes remarkably little effort and can yield substantial results. After all, it doesn't take a lot of time or trouble to exchange telephone numbers, yet when you are working at home in the evening and have a problem, that telephone number may be the difference between wasting an hour working something out wrong, when a little help would have saved you so much.

6.3 Using external support

As well as the support available from your employment and your Centre, there are other sources you can draw on. We have already mentioned public libraries, as a useful resource, as somewhere to work in peace and quiet, and also as a source of books and journals for following up extensions. If you live in a larger town or city, the library may offer a substantial resource to learners like you, but even a small branch library can be just the place to think and reflect without too many distractions.

Even if you are not enrolled there, you will probably be able to use the library at your local college or university, if there is one locally. You should introduce yourself at the desk and ask if you might use their facilities, without borrowing books; it would be very unusual for your request to be refused, unless there is a shortage of space at a particular period.

Some TECs (Training and Enterprise Councils) in England and Wales or LECs (Local Enterprise Companies) in Scotland have set up local networks and forums for people on management development programmes, particularly those working towards S/NVQs. Your Centre should be able to help you to find out about these – they may even host one. The value of such networks is that you can meet people from a wide range of organizations and roles, and find that you learn an awful lot from them, just through informal meetings.

Finally, don't forget that your friends and relatives can also be a source of help. Sometimes it is difficult to see how much help is available locally, and you could be looking for professional support when there is adequate advice available downstairs, next door or round the corner. Choose wisely, of course, but don't ignore what is there.

6.4 Support from NEBS Management

As we have already pointed out, NEBS Management is the UK's largest provider of management qualifications, and its support services are a valuable part of the service it offers. These are mainly there to support the Centre, so you won't necessarily be aware of them, except that they will send in a verifier to the Centre to check the quality of the assessment and ensure that you are being assessed fairly.

Because NEBS Management is there, your Centre is able to offer you access to the sort of learning opportunities that you require, including of course, Super Series! The NEBS Management Regional Manager will visit the Centre regularly and you will be registered with NEBS Management early on in your programme. If you encounter any problems with your programme – in the way that you are supported or assessed – the Centre will have arrangements for you to register your concerns and, if necessary, appeal against any assessment decisions that are made.

This is a requirement of the approval of the Centre, and if you feel that it is necessary, you can eventually appeal any assessment decision to NEBS Management itself. Why should this happen? In practice it hardly ever does, but the quality of support which NEBS Management ensures is in place through its approval system is designed to cover all eventualities. If you need to contact them for any reason, you can do so by writing to:

> NEBS Management
> 1, Giltspur Street
> London
> EC1A 9DD

You can telephone them on:

> 0171 294 2470

and fax them on:

> 0171 294 2402

6.5 Taking your personal development further

You may feel that, having just set out on your new programme, now is not the time to contemplate where you go afterwards, but by the time you complete it you will need to be thinking about your future development. At this point you might just like to think about the possibilities that are open to you. If you are following the capability route, you can continue up it, moving from the Introductory Award to the full Certificate, from there or from the Introductory Diploma to the full Diploma. If you are on the competence route you can follow that up from S/NVQ Level 3 to Level 4 or from Level 4 to Level 5.

However, you are not obliged to stick with one route; many people will choose to start with, say, a NEBS Management Certificate (or Introductory Award) and build up a portfolio based on the assignments they have completed there to achieve a S/NVQ at Level 3 or 4, according to their job role and opportunities to gather evidence. The same is true with the NEBS Management Diploma (or Introductory Diploma); you can build on that to gain a S/NVQ at Level 4 or Level 5.

The following diagram illustrates the various routes open to you. Now is a good time to think about this, especially if you want to move from a capability qualification to a S/NVQ, because the way you undertake your assignments and collect them together can determine how far down the road you are to your S/NVQ portfolio. So, talk to your Centre's staff about the possibilities and your own personal goals.

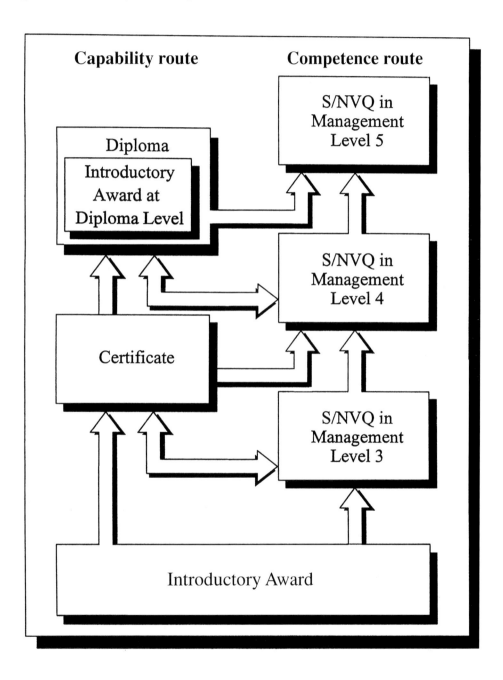

Appendix I Summary of workbook contents

A Managing Activities

1 *Planning and Controlling Work*
Why do managers need to plan, how do they and their organizations benefit from plans and the planning process? You will learn how to develop plans which can help you to monitor and control your team's work and achieve targets for output and quality, within the resources available.

2 *Understanding Quality*
Customers are concerned more than ever before about quality, and improving quality can bring both competitive advantages and real gains in the efficiency of operations. You will learn about the different approaches to quality management and some of the techniques you can use to lead your team in the quality improvement process.

3 *Achieving Quality*
This workbook takes you further into the details of quality improvement and the implementation of quality management systems. It introduces you to some of the specialized techniques of monitoring output quality, quality control and quality improvement.

4 *Auditing Quality*
Formal performance standards need to be measured periodically to ensure they are maintained. This book describes different kinds of quality audit then takes you through the process of planning, preparing, carrying out an audit, reporting back and dealing with any resulting non-compliance. It is seen from the perspective of first line managers who may be using audit techniques to maintain quality in their own area or may be providing information and motivating workteams to co-operate with an audit team.

5 *Caring for the Customer*
Customer care makes the difference between meeting customer requirements and delighting them, ensuring that they return again and again. You will learn how to identify both internal and external customers, find out their requirements and develop your team's performance to meet and then exceed those requirements.

55

6 *Marketing and Selling*
Any organization's survival depends on its ability to satisfy its customers. The core concept of marketing is to be able to see the organization the way your customers see it. This workbook will enable you to identify your customers, appreciate how they view you and your products or services, what they expect from your organization, and how to satisfy them successfully.

7 *Managing a Safe Environment*
Organizations operate under tight regulations to ensure that they operate safely. Using this workbook will help you in understanding the systems that employers have in place to ensure and improve safety, and your role in ensuring that the legislation is complied with is an essential requirement for every manager.

8 *Managing Lawfully – Health, Safety and Environment*
Legislation from the UK Government and from the European Union is designed to ensure that organizations provide a safe and healthy environment and products for their employees, customers and the local community and don't pollute the wider environment in which they operate. This workbook helps you to understand the legislative framework and makes it easier for you to use internal systems and structures to identify potential problems and avoid them.

9 *Preventing Accidents*
Accidents occur because people don't foresee the potential outcomes of their actions. Preventing accidents is more than just avoiding obvious risks, and this workbook introduces you to the skills and knowledge required to assess possible causes of accidents, build in measures to prevent them occurring and how to deal with them if they do occur.

10 *Leading Change*
Why is change necessary and why can it be so difficult? This workbook helps you to understand the reasons for change, identify likely future changes, appreciate why change is resisted and how to overcome resistance. You will learn that change is not something you implement and then forget; you will see it as a continuous activity and learn how to welcome it and make it happen smoothly and effectively.

B Managing Resources

1 *Controlling Physical Resources*
People, facilities, machinery, equipment, components and materials – these are the basis for all productive operations and the role of the first line manager is primarily about deploying these resources and supervising their performance. In this workbook you will learn how to employ the techniques which can help you to achieve the most effective use of the physical assets and personnel available.

2 *Managing Energy Efficiency*

This book suggests methods and techniques to improve energy efficiency through changing methods or through changing attitudes and behaviour. It reviews the background and principles of energy efficiency and the impact an energy management programme can have on Total Quality Management. It suggests a five-point strategy for improving energy efficiency which can be implemented at an organizational level or, in a very practical way, within your own area of responsibility.

3 *Improving Efficiency*

Improved efficiency is not an option for any organization; increasing competition in the public and voluntary sectors as well as the private sector makes the pressure to produce more with less an imperative. This workbook will help you to understand what efficiency means in your organization, and how we can measure resource efficiency and redeploy resources to maximize efficiency.

4 *Understanding Finance*

Finance is not something to be left to accountants. All managers must be able to budget for the future, control costs and assess organizational performance. This workbook will help you to understand the basic principles of financial management, recognize the role and importance of financial control, and analyse common financial documents and determine the financial welfare of an organization.

5 *Working with Budgets*

Drawing up and controlling a budget is a key skill for an effective manager, as budgets are the mechanism through which the utilization of all resources can be forecast and monitored. This workbook will provide you with the knowledge and skills required to ensure that resources are deployed as planned and any variations are identified and accounted for.

6 *Controlling Costs*

Success or failure in any organization depends upon effective control of costs. This means knowing the value of the resources being deployed, comparing this to the planned level of expenditure, detecting any variation and its causes, recommending action to rectify the situation and identifying the implications for the organization. This workbook will enable you to understand the processes involved and utilize the techniques of effective cost control.

7 *Making a Financial Case*

As increasing responsibility is passed down to the lower management levels, so is the need to make sound business cases to support requests for resources for their own areas of responsibility. It is no longer the sole province of senior managers. This workbook will enable you to carry out such an analysis and to present a coherent argument based on realistic forecasts of expenditure and revenue. It will also help with the NEBS Management Certificate project.

C Managing People

1 *How Organizations Work*

Organizations are complex social structures, different personalities filling a variety of different roles in formal and informal relationships with each other. Understanding the legal structure – public or private limited company, public or voluntary sector organization – provides a starting point for analysing structures, authority, control, culture and communication. This workbook will help you to understand your organization and the organizations that you come into contact with.

2 *Managing with Authority*

Having the authority to manage properly is essential. In this workbook you will understand more about authority and how it is established and used in your workplace, be able to distinguish between different kinds of authority and be given help to use your authority effectively to the benefit of your team and your organization.

3 *Leading Your Team*

Leadership is different from management or supervision, although it is dependent upon it. Leadership requires that you can provide your team members with a clear sense of direction and the confidence to achieve the objectives set for them. This workbook will show you how you can develop your management style to become an effective team leader and contribute to the achievement of your organization's overall goals.

4 *Delegating Effectively*

If you want something done well, do it yourself! If you have ever felt that, then you need to consider how good your delegation skills are. This workbook provides you with the knowledge required to assess which tasks you should perform and which can be delegated, to select those people to whom tasks should be delegated, and the skills needed to delegate effectively.

5 *Working in Teams*

Teams are more than just random groups of people pulled together to undertake particular tasks. This workbook will help you to identify what makes a good team and to learn how to create an effective team from the group of people that you lead. In the process you will have a chance to assess yourself and your team's role and performance and work on ways of developing both.

6 *Motivating People*

You can drive people to work faster, you can control them so that they work for longer, but as soon as you turn your back can you rely upon them to maintain the standards that you have enforced? *Motivating People* will show you how you can create a team which performs better without the need for your constant supervision, a team where innovation and improvement are possible.

7 *Securing the Right People*

Any workteam works better if it contains the right people for the tasks required to be performed. This workbook offers a practical approach to the techniques you can use to recruit, select and maintain team members once they are appointed.

8 *Appraising Performance*

How well do members of your workteam perform? Formal appraisal can be a powerful force for change and improvement in an organization – equally it can be threatening, bureaucratic and disdained. This workbook will show you how an appraisal system can work to your and your team's benefit, developing your understanding of the process and your skills in conducting appraisal interviews.

9 *Planning Training and Development*

All organizations depend on their employees for their success, and Investors in People has taught us that employees must be invested in if they are to perform to the standards demanded by the increasingly competitive markets in which you operate. This workbook will help you to identify the training and development needs of the members of your team and the most appropriate way of meeting those needs.

10 *Delivering Training*

Increasing numbers of employers are looking to supervisors/first line managers to take an active role, not just in identifying training and development needs, but in delivering the training required. From informal, on the job coaching to formal, off the job training sessions, this workbook will give you the skills and the confidence to pass on your expertise to others.

11 *Managing Lawfully – People and Employment*

All employees have rights, the most common cause of infringement of those rights is ignorance, and ignorance costs employers dear. This workbook will make you aware of your responsibilities, as a manager, for ensuring that those rights are adhered to and that, when action must be taken about employees, it is done in a way that respects those rights whilst achieving the desired outcome fairly and equitably.

12 *Commitment to Equality*

Why is equality important? There are moral, legal and economic reasons for ensuring that employees and others are treated equitably. This workbook will help you understand your responsibilities for ensuring that equity is achieved in your workplace, treating people in the way that they have a right to expect, adhering to the legislation that protects those rights, and avoiding the diseconomies that occur because the wrong people are employed or customers are insulted, through prejudice and ignorance.

13 *Becoming More Effective*

The only person with complete responsibility for your development and performance is you. This workbook will show you how you can take control of your development and achieve the goals that you have set for yourself. It will enable you to transform your performance, translating what you have learnt into your everyday practice, and so become more effective.

14 *Managing Tough Times*

Times are tough; delayering, downsizing, and all the other euphemisms for employing fewer people but expecting them to do more, mean only one thing for supervisors and first line managers – the job gets harder! But you can learn how to cope with these pressures, and turn the threats into real opportunities for yourself and your workteam. *Managing Tough Times* offers you the skills and the knowledge you require to put some order and control into the complex and chaotic world that so many organizations now face.

15 *Managing Time*

Time is the one resource we all use – what's more we use it whether we want to or not. You can't save time, you can't speed it up, but what you can do is manage it, to get the maximum benefit from the time that's available. This workbook will enable you to learn how to use your time better, setting priorities and allocating your workload in a way that makes the most of your most precious resource.

D Managing Information

1 *Collecting Information*

Information is increasingly being recognized as one of the most significant assets of any organization, yet without effective collection and storage, it is of no value or use. This workbook will help you to recognize the different types and sources of information, the different formats and methodologies for collecting it, and to select the most appropriate of these for the information and its subsequent storage, analysis and use.

2 *Storing and Retrieving Information*

Holding information in a format in which it can't be used is a waste of money and a source of danger to an organization. This workbook will help you to identify the most appropriate medium for storing information, in the light of its format, importance, sensitivity and subsequent use, and the security and legal aspects which should be taken into account when deciding on storage and retrieval systems.

3 *Information in Management*

This is the third workbook in the group related to information. It's reasonable to assume that once collected, stored and retrieved information only becomes useful when it starts being used. This workbook helps you to analyse, interpret, present and evaluate meaningful information using both manual and computer-aided techniques.

4 *Communication in Management*

Communication is an essential element of any organization, from the informal meeting in the corridor or shopfloor, to the formal meeting with agenda and minutes. This workbook will help you to understand the role of good communication in management, how to recognize communication failures and how to improve the quality of communication between those you manage and with others inside and outside the organization.

5 *Listening and Speaking*

Communicating is something we all possess, to some degree or another, even though it requires a complex mix of skills and practice. We learn to read and write from a very early age but speaking and listening (especially the latter) does not always come so naturally, This workbook concentrates on these two particular personal communication skills and takes you through step by step to help you improve and apply these skills to your daily management activities.

6 *Communicating in Groups*

A particular aspect of effective management communication is the ability to communicate with and to a group of individuals. In this workbook you will explore how to be active and capable in meetings and to plan, prepare and deliver an effective speech or presentation.

7 *Writing Effectively*

When should you write, and when should you speak to somebody? What makes an effective letter, memo or set of minutes? How do you ensure that what you intended to convey is understood by the recipient of your written communication? This workbook will increase your skills and your confidence in putting words on paper, and help you to recognize effective writing in the work of others.

8 *Project and Report Writing*

Essential for anybody working towards the NEBS Management Certificate, but valuable for anybody who has to keep proper records of projects or make a case to others for their decision. This workbook will show you how to structure your material, what to put in (and what to leave out), the appropriate style to adopt, and how to use clear, understandable English.

9 *Making and Taking Decisions*

Good managers make decisions, the best managers make the right decisions (most of the time)! There is no simple way of ensuring that you always get it right, but there are ways of improving your decision-making which will give you greater confidence whilst at the same time reducing the pressure that you feel when you are faced with complex and significant decisions. This workbook introduces a range of techniques which you can use to assist you in your decision-making and help you make the right decisions, and make them stick.

10 *Solving Problems*

If organizations didn't have problems, they wouldn't need managers. Your role is to ensure that the number of problems is minimized, but when they do occur, you should approach them in a structured and analytical way, so that their causes are identified and real solutions are adopted. This workbook shows you how to employ a range of techniques for problem analysis and solution, and to ensure that your solution can be implemented successfully.

Appendix 2 Summary of audio cassette contents

1 Reaching Decisions

Managers have to reach decisions, that's what being a manager is all about. On this cassette you will hear managers talking about the problems that they face and the sort of decisions that they have to reach. They argue that your role is to manage the decision-making process, which can involve you in encouraging others to reach decisions, rather than letting them 'dump' them all on you. It also means watching out for the problems that will present you with urgent decisions, or with a limited range of options, when earlier action could have avoided crisis behaviour.

A good manager uses other people for advice and help in reaching decisions, and involves workteams in the process as much as possible, not to avoid responsibility, but to ensure that the right decisions are made, leading to actions which will work to resolve problems and achieve objectives. The managers featured on the cassette argue that the way you reach decisions is as important as the decisions themselves, and that you need to think long term and ensure consistency in your decisions so that you control the consequences of the decision-making process.

This cassette contains four question breaks, as follows:

Break 1:   How well are you managing the function of reaching decisions?

Break 2:   Are you making the best use of the support you could get from senior managers and technical experts?

Break 3:   How successfully do you involve your team in taking and owning decisions?

Break 4:   How confident are you that your decisions are going to work in the long term?

Reaching Decisions complements the following workbooks:

■ *Making and Taking Decisions*
■ *Solving Problems*

2 Managing the Bottom Line

This cassette introduces you to managers who have had to make some critical budgetary decisions about the way their part of the organization operates, in order to achieve their financial goals. It doesn't matter whether you operate in the private, public or voluntary sector; as these managers talk about these budgetary decisions you will see how impossible it is to separate operational accountability (what you and your team do and how they do it) from financial accountability (the effect this has on costs and revenues). You will also hear how delegation of budgets opens up a greater range of opportunities for managers, as well as bringing greater responsibility, and that it is possible to substitute increased revenue for reduced costs in balancing the budget and managing the bottom line.

This cassette contains three question breaks, as follows:

Break 1: How can you think creatively about cost improvements?

Break 2: Do the financial cases you are currently making deliver cost benefits and match your manager's business plans and priorities?

Break 3: How can you build the right team to work with you on a cost-saving project?

Managing the Bottom Line complements the following workbooks:

- *Controlling Costs*
- *Making a Financial Case*
- *Working with Budgets*

3 Customers Count

No matter how good the product is that you are selling, without a real concern for the customer you cannot be certain of success. The managers you will hear in this cassette talk about the need to understand your customers and to set out not just to satisfy them but to delight them with a service that exceeds their expectations. This means looking at all aspects of your customer care, including the location, the environment and the times at which your customers can receive the product or service.

To ensure that you understand your customers and their concerns you need to find out about them and help them to communicate with you. You will hear how making it easy for customers to complain – and taking those complaints seriously – has helped organizations to improve their services. These managers see customer care as being far more than saying 'Have a nice day'; for them it is the fact that the whole organization must be really concerned for customers to ensure its long-term success.

This cassette contains six question breaks, as follows:

Break 1: Do you and your organization see things from the customers' point of view? Could you do more?

Break 2: What can you do to make your product or service more attractive to new and existing customers?

Break 3: Is doing business an enjoyable experience for your customers?

Break 4: Are you selling the right product or service from the right place?

Break 5: What information do you have about or from your customers?

Break 6: How successfully do you 'infect' your workteam with the need for better customer care?

Customers Count complements the following workbooks:

■ *Caring for the Customer*
■ *Understanding Quality*

4 Being the Best

There is an important difference between wanting to do well and actually being the best. No serious manager likes under-performing, but it is often hard to recognize areas where we need to improve, just as it is difficult sometimes to see our real strengths. This cassette encourages you to look at the way you manage and to actively review your performance; other managers have done this, and you can hear what it means to take control of your own development. It is easy sometimes to criticize others for not doing what we expect of them, but sometimes that is easier than reflecting on our own weaknesses. We have to recognize that, as a manager, we determine the effectiveness of the individuals and workteams that we manage – our strengths and weaknesses are often reflected in their performance. That's why we need the skills and knowledge that ensure we can get the best from others.

But when you listen to the managers on the cassette, you will also be encouraged to think about the personal impact of coping with the increasing demands that the modern workplace puts on you. 'Being the best' is not just about skills and strategies, it is also about ensuring that you are capable of balancing the different compartments of your life effectively.

This cassette contains four question breaks, as follows:

Break 1: Have you a development strategy for yourself as a manager? How do you rate your management skills and your credibility?

Break 2: Does your delegation achieve results for you, your workteam and your organization?

Break 3:   How good are you at planning?

Break 4:   How do you control stress?

Being the Best complements the following workbooks:

- *Becoming More Effective*
- *Delegating Effectively*
- *Managing Time*
- *Managing Tough Times*

5 Working Together

This cassette looks at three interrelated elements – the individual, the team and the task – to consider your role in achieving your own and your workteam's objectives. The managers you will hear present the different strategies that they use to motivate individuals to work well, and to get teams working together to ensure that tasks are completed effectively. You are encouraged to think about your own preferences and the way that your workteam behave to achieve effective working.

The most challenging problem for any manager is getting the best possible performance from individuals. Issues such as leadership, motivation, control and delegation are all important; different managers use them in different ways to maximize the performance of their team members. You need to make your own decisions, but by listening to the views of other managers you will have a clearer idea of what will work best for you.

This cassette contains four question breaks, as follows:

Break 1:   What motivates you and your team? If praise was among the things you thought of, do you give praise often enough to make a difference?

Break 2:   How do you manage problem people?

Break 3:   How can you get your people to function more effectively?

Break 4:   How does your team know where they are headed? They may know what you want, but do you know what they want?

Working Together complements the following workbooks:

- *Leading Your Team*
- *Working in Teams*
- *Motivating People*

65

Appendix 3 Sources of general help and advice

Name	What are they?	Address	Telephone and URL
The Qualifications and Curriculum Authority	During 1997 QCA replaced NCVQ in having responsibility for overseeing all qualifications, especially NVQs, used in England, Wales and Northern Ireland	c/o NCVQ 222, Euston Road London NW1 2BZ	0171 387 9898
The Scottish Qualifications Authority	SQA has responsibility for overseeing all qualifications used in Scotland	Hanover House 24 Douglas Street Glasgow G2 7NQ	0141 248 7900
The Management Charter Initiative	MCI is the operating arm of the lead body responsible for developing the standards for management S/NVQs	Russell Square House London WC1 5BR	0171 872 9000 www.bbi.co.uk/mci
The British Association for Open Learning	BAOL members are involved in developing, promoting and using open learning	Suite 16, Pixmore House Pixmore Avenue Letchworth Hertfordshire SG6 1JG	01462 485588
The National Council for Educational Technology	NCET helps centres to use information technology to support learning	Milburn Hill Road Science Park Coventry CV4 7JJ	01203 416994 www.ncet.org.uk
The Scottish Council for Educational Technology	SCET helps centres in Scotland to use information technology to support learning	74 Victoria Crescent Road Glasgow G12 9JN	0141 337 5000 www.scet.org.uk

SUPER SERIES

SUPER SERIES 3

0-7506-3362-X   Full Set of Workbooks, User Guide and Support Guide

A. Managing Activities

0-7506-3295-X	1. Planning and Controlling Work
0-7506-3296-8	2. Understanding Quality
0-7506-3297-6	3. Achieving Quality
0-7506-3298-4	4. Caring for the Customer
0-7506-3299-2	5. Marketing and Selling
0-7506-3300-X	6. Managing a Safe Environment
0-7506-3301-8	7. Managing Lawfully - Health, Safety and Environment
0-7506-37064	8. Preventing Accidents
0-7506-3302-6	9. Leading Change
0-7506-4091-X	10. Auditing Quality

B. Managing Resources

0-7506-3303-4	1. Controlling Physical Resources
0-7506-3304-2	2. Improving Efficiency
0-7506-3305-0	3. Understanding Finance
0-7506-3306-9	4. Working with Budgets
0-7506-3307-7	5. Controlling Costs
0-7506-3308-5	6. Making a Financial Case
0-7506-4092-8	7. Managing Energy Efficiency

C. Managing People

0-7506-3309-3	1. How Organisations Work
0-7506-3310-7	2. Managing with Authority
0-7506-3311-5	3. Leading Your Team
0-7506-3312-3	4. Delegating Effectively
0-7506-3313-1	5. Working in Teams
0-7506-3314-X	6. Motivating People
0-7506-3315-8	7. Securing the Right People
0-7506-3316-6	8. Appraising Performance
0-7506-3317-4	9. Planning Training and Development
0-75063318-2	10. Delivering Training
0-7506-3320-4	11. Managing Lawfully - People and Employment
0-7506-3321-2	12. Commitment to Equality
0-7506-3322-0	13. Becoming More Effective
0-7506-3323-9	14. Managing Tough Times
0-7506-3324-7	15. Managing Time

D. Managing Information

0-7506-3325-5	1. Collecting Information
0-7506-3326-3	2. Storing and Retrieving Information
0-7506-3327-1	3. Information in Management
0-7506-3328-X	4. Communication in Management
0-7506-3329-8	5. Listening and Speaking
0-7506-3330-1	6. Communicating in Groups
0-7506-3331-X	7. Writing Effectively
0-7506-3332-8	8. Project and Report Writing
0-7506-3333-6	9. Making and Taking Decisions
0-7506-3334-4	10. Solving Problems

SUPER SERIES 3 USER GUIDE + SUPPORT GUIDE

0-7506-37056	1. User Guide
0-7506-37048	2. Support Guide

SUPER SERIES 3 CASSETTE TITLES

0-7506-3707-2	1. Complete Cassette Pack
0-7506-3711-0	2. Reaching Decisions
0-7506-3712-9	3. Making a Financial Case
0-7506-3710-2	4. Customers Count
0-7506-3709-9	5. Being the Best
0-7506-3708-0	6. Working Together

To Order - phone us direct for prices and availability details
(please quote ISBNs when ordering)
College orders: 01865 314333 • Account holders: 01865 314301
Individual purchases: 01865 314627 (please have credit card details ready)